Teachers Do Make a Difference

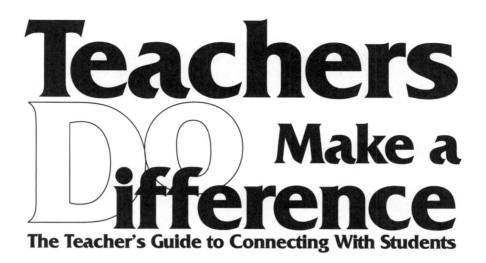

Teachers Do Make a Difference

The Teacher's Guide to Connecting With Students

Judith A. Deiro
Foreword by Bonnie Benard

CORWIN PRESS
A Sage Publications Company
Thousand Oaks, California

For information:

Corwin Press
A Sage Publications Company
2455 Teller Road
Thousand Oaks, California 91320
www.corwinpress.com

Sage Publications Ltd.
1 Oliver's Yard
55 City Road
London EC1Y 1SP
United Kingdom

Sage Publications India Pvt. Ltd.
B-42, Panchsheel Enclave
Post Box 4109
New Delhi 110 017 India

Printed in the United States of America

Library of Congress Cataloging-in-Publication Data

Deiro, Judith A.
Teachers *do* make a difference: The teacher's guide to connecting with students / Judith A. Deiro.
       p. cm.
Includes bibliographical references and index.
ISBN 1-4129-0653-9 (cloth) — ISBN 1-4129-0654-7 (pbk.)
   1. Teacher-student relationships—United States. 2. Teachers—United States.
3. Teaching—United States. I. Title.
LB1033.D435 2005
371.102′3—dc22
                                           2004007967

This book is printed on acid-free paper.

04   05   06   07   10   9   8   7   6   5   4   3   2   1

Acquisitions Editor:	Faye Zucker
Editorial Assistant:	Stacy Wagner
Production Editor:	Denise Santoyo
Copy Editor:	Diana Breti
Typesetter:	C&M Digitals (P) Ltd.
Cover Designer:	Anthony Paular

Contents

Foreword

Throughout my reading of *Teachers DO Make a Difference*, I found myself continually feeling gratitude—gratitude for the heart and humanity of the six wonderful teachers described in this book, who are indeed making a difference in the lives of the youth in their care, and gratitude for my friend and colleague Judy Deiro, for capturing and recording their voices. Lastly, my deep gratitude goes out to you, the readers (and teachers), who care enough about young people to pick up this book in the midst of your overwhelmingly busy lives. You will not be disappointed. In fact, you will be affirmed and invigorated.

I have spent the last twenty years seeking to understand and identify factors that protect young people from high-risk behaviors, including school failure and dropping out. I heartily concur with the theme of Judy's book: establishing caring, respectful, inviting relationships with young people *is* the bottom line for promoting their healthy emotional and social development *and* the number one prerequisite for student learning.

"He knew I had a lot of problems, but he always believed I was a good person and could do good things. I credit him with my life. Without his belief in me, I couldn't have stopped doing the things I was doing." These are the words of one of the teachers in this book, describing a teacher who made a difference in his own life. The teacher's words echo what thousands of young people growing up in high-risk environments have told us in interviews, in qualitative studies of turnaround schools, and in longitudinal developmental research about the power of a nurturing teacher, classroom, and school to transform their life experience from despair to hope and from chaos to meaning.

Judy's book, more than any other I have read over my many years in prevention and education, encapsulates precisely what teachers are able to do to support both the healthy development and successful learning of their students, even those students dealing with multiple challenges and adversities. Judy identifies the specific practices and beliefs of teachers who make a difference—teachers who motivate and engage *all* their students, especially "those students" that others have given up on. Through actual classroom vignettes, Judy paints a picture of what caring, respect, and invitational relationships look like. She then ties these classroom portraits directly to the principles of practice that they illustrate.

The book you hold in your hands conveys *good* news: "closing the achievement gap" and creating "high-performing" schools depends not on *what* we teach but *how* we teach. Judy Deiro clearly shows that schools do not need yet another curriculum, but rather positive adult-student connections as well as caring and respectful learning communities in our classrooms. The challenge to all caring educators in this age of high-stakes testing and one-size-fits-all standards is to get the message of this book out to preservice and practicing teachers and administrators, to educational policymakers, and to the general public: *All students can learn, relationships matter, and teachers DO make a difference!*

—*Bonnie Benard*
Health and Human Development Program, WestEd, CA

Preface

Anxiously I sat at the end of a large conference table surrounded by the five university professors on my doctoral dissertation committee. I had planned well for this day. I had strategically obtained feedback on my research methodology and writing from everyone on my committee—everyone except "Dr. Smith." Every time I asked her for feedback, she was too busy to get back to me in a timely manner. I had wanted to make sure every committee member approved of what I was doing as I moved through the dissertation process because I had chosen an unorthodox topic to explore empirically: what teachers do to nurture bonding with students.

Now the completed dissertation, a tome of 418 pages, lay before each of the committee members. The first time "Dr. Smith" had ever seen any part of my dissertation was this week. Nervously, I glanced at her. I had no idea what her reaction would be and I knew a negative response from her could block my graduation.

My dissertation chair opened the meeting. After I gave a ten-minute opening presentation on my research methodology and the results, he asked if there were any questions. "Dr. Smith" immediately said, "Yes, I want to be the first to speak." My heart began to pound. She did not look at me but stared at the other committee members and continued, "Because I have not had a chance to look at this dissertation until this week, I have been reading it every night. Last night I even dreamt about it." She paused and softly laughed. "It is quite inspirational," she added.

Then turning and looking directly at me, she said, "Judy, I have one question for you. Have you gone back to thank the teacher who made a difference for you?" I was stunned. I began to stammer, trying to think of an appropriate response. Finally, I simply admitted I hadn't. "Dr. Smith" responded, "I haven't either, but after reading your dissertation, I plan to."

The next day I was on the phone, tracing down Mr. Charles Booth, the English teacher who had made a difference for me. You see, at a poignant time in my senior year he had said just a few words to me that I hung onto for years. It was not the result of any lengthy connection or intense involvement. I was not even sure he would remember who I was after thirty years! And I knew, for sure, he would not know what he had done, although the few words spoken meant the world to me. Because of my research, I now understood why those few words carried such persuasive power and made such a difference for me. I had always respected Mr. Booth throughout my four years in high school. And he had always treated me, and all students, with respect and dignity. I knew that I had to let him know how I felt.

I did get in touch with Mr. Booth, and thanked him for the very meaningful and significant role he had played in my young life. As always, he was gracious and wise. I have asked him to share with you his thoughts about our conversation and making a difference as a teacher.

Mr. Booth's Reaction

Recently one of my former students, Judy Deiro, tracked me down to tell me that I had somehow made a significant contribution to her development and career. Speaking with her brought forth a flood of beautiful memories and a tremendous feeling of accomplishment and closure. Judy made it clear that as her teacher, I had made a difference in her life. Yes, I did remember her . . . but I did not recall doing anything out of the ordinary for her when she was my student.

As a classroom teacher, my hope was to always help my students develop in as many ways as possible. I, of course, remained devoted to their mastery of important subject matter, but I wanted much more for them. Over time, my students would become more and more an essential part of my personal and professional experience. Their successes, failures, frustrations, and growth became personalized within our relationship. As each student graduated and moved on, I could not but wonder whether I had, in any substantial way, made a difference. Judy's call to me, after thirty years of not hearing from her, was a wonderful affirmation of many years of hard work well spent. I wish every educator could enjoy such wonderful feedback. Teachers do make a difference.

A LITTLE BOOK FOR BUSY TEACHERS

The little book you hold in your hands is a follow up to a longer book, *Teaching With Heart,* that I wrote immediately after completing my dissertation. This new book is written for the busy educator who does not have the time or energy to read the longer book, but wants to understand how he or she can make a difference for students. Backed by research, this book tells just what teachers do to make that difference. And even more important, it affirms that we *can* make a difference without adding more responsibilities to our already busy schedules, or going beyond the expectations of our job descriptions as teachers.

The relationship we develop with our students is the heart of how we make changes in student lives. Research clearly shows that it is the relationship—a meaningful, healthy connection with students—that promotes prosocial, responsible behavior among students. This book offers specific suggestions for building those meaningful connections in simple and appropriate ways. It debunks common myths about what we have to do and who we have to be to make a difference. This book provides important principles for building close and trusting relationships with students. Along with the principles for caring, it provides real-life exemplars and vignettes of six caring teachers practicing those principles.

OVERVIEW

In Chapter 1, I verify that the most powerful and effective way teachers can help students overcome the harmful influences they deal with in their environments is by developing close and caring connections with them. Using research, I document that the healthy emotional and social development of children in today's society is dependent on having more caring adults meaningfully involved in their lives. In Chapter 2, I describe different strategies for making healthy connections with students, using exemplars from the six caring teachers I observed during my dissertation research. In Chapter 3, I discuss what teachers do to help students perceive our caring. In Chapter 4, I describe what personal resources and strategies we need to maintain our enthusiasm and professional energy, which can easily be depleted by working so intensely with students. In Chapter 5, I conclude with my thoughts and responses to some major concerns raised by different teachers regarding making healthy connections with students. And finally, in the appendices of the book, I give you more examples directly from my data highlighting the personal resources or qualities discussed as exemplified by *each* of the teachers.

MAKING A DIFFERENCE

For all teachers, I know the information in this book gives us some new ways to think about how to make meaningful, inviting, caring connections with our students and different ways to think about our student relationships in general. For teachers working hard to engage students who are preoccupied with personal worries, I know we will find some affirmation and validation for our heartfelt efforts. For student teachers struggling to develop connections with students while still learning how to teach your subject content, I hope you are encouraged to continue your efforts to develop a teaching style that naturally integrates these two primary responsibilities of a teacher. I want to affirm that your goal is possible and you have chosen the right career. And finally, for those of us who are prevention specialists and responsible for intervening and preventing high-risk behaviors among students, I know this little book will reframe how teachers can be effectively involved in our school prevention efforts.

Finally, as you read this book I hope you too will be motivated to go back and thank the teacher who made a difference for you! As I disclosed in the vignette at the beginning of this Preface, I did. And "Dr. Smith" did too. For me, it was an emotionally touching moment that gave me a sense of completion. And as an added, unexpected benefit, I again have in my life the remarkable person who once made a difference for me.

ACKNOWLEDGMENTS

First and foremost, I want to thank the six caring teachers for graciously giving me the opportunity to observe them while they were teaching and relating to students. Doing the research for my dissertation is still a vivid memory for me. Observing their commitment, dedication, and high regard for students and the teaching profession was pure joy. Out of courtesy, I do not use their real names, or the real names of anyone introduced in the text.

I also want to express my appreciation and gratitude to several individuals who spent a significant amount of time editing drafts of this book and giving me valuable feedback: Georgeanne Brown and Sherrie Fulton, two retired K–12 teachers with more than fifty years of teaching experience between them, gave valuable insights that helped ground and shape this book during its evolution. Patricia Nerison, retired English professor and poet, who at the drop of a hat edited the penultimate draft and eased my fears and self-doubts. I also want to thank Bonnie Benard, whose belief in me and all teachers is awe inspiring. Finally, I want to thank Dr. Michael Knapp, the chair of my dissertation committee, who exemplifies what this book is about. His enthusiasm for the findings and sincere desire to see them published encouraged me to continue writing.

A special thanks to Faye Zucker, Stacy Wagner, Diana Breti, and Denise Santoyo at Corwin Press for all the work they did to make this book a reality.

About the Author

Judith A. Deiro, PhD, has worked as a teacher, counselor, and an education consultant for more than thirty-four years. Since 1997 she has been teaching full time at Western Washington University in the Human Services program. During her professional career she has worked as a vocational rehabilitation counselor, state women's prison counselor, chemical dependency counselor in an outpatient treatment center, and full-time postsecondary education teacher and counselor. She has received the Full-Time Faculty Excellence Award; Chemical Dependency Educator of the Year; and the Award for Excellence Among Women by Association of Women in Community and Junior Colleges, Washington State Chapter. As an education consultant, she has given numerous presentations nationwide on healthy teaching and parenting strategies for the prevention of high-risk behaviors.

Judy's keen scholarly interest in the roles teachers play in child development led her to write the book *Teaching With Heart* (1996). That book and this new companion volume offer teachers research-based and teacher-tested ways to make healthy connections with their students. Judy hopes her books will encourage teachers to develop the close and caring connections that facilitate healthy social and emotional development in young people.

Bonnie Benard is Senior Program Associate for the Health and Human Development Program at WestEd in Oakland, California. She is the author of *Resiliency: What We Have Learned* (2004).

1

Our Changing Roles as Teachers

It is very late in the afternoon, way beyond the end of the school day at Suburb Junior High School. Richard, a seasoned counselor, slips inside the doorway of the seventh-grade Social Studies classroom and collapses against the wall with a heavy sigh. Pam, the teacher, is chatting with me, tidying up, and getting ready to go home. I have been interviewing Pam for a qualitative study on caring teachers.

From across the room Pam looks at the fifty-five-year-old bearded and balding counselor and empathetically says, "Rough day, huh Richard?" Pam is aware Richard has been working with an eighth-grade student who lost a dear friend to suicide that morning. The suicide victim had been the girl's neighbor and surrogate parent for years. While still in bed, he put a gun to his head and pulled the trigger. Understandably, the young teenager was distraught, confused, and felt betrayed by the behavior of someone she respected, trusted, and relied upon. Richard has just spent the entire day working with her and the other students affected. In between, he continued to handle his regularly scheduled appointments and responsibilities.

While listening to the exchange between Richard and Pam, I am reminded of how emotionally draining it is to be bombarded continually with the problems of young people in distress. I know Richard's entire schedule had been suddenly turned upside down in response to this student's needs. He had to get in touch with the student's parents to make sure they knew what to look for in their daughter's reaction, find a grief counselor to work pro bono with the girl over the next couple of weeks, notify all the teachers of her situation and ask them to be alert to other students who knew this community member and may be in shock over the incident. And Richard had to do this while handling other student crises that are part of a normal day for a middle school counselor. As I watch Pam listen empathetically to Richard, I realize that most people have no idea what schools cope with on a daily basis. While the general public decries the low achievement scores of students and asserts the need to "fix" our schools, every day teachers are dealing with students emotionally distressed and preoccupied with difficult personal situations such as absentee parents, blended-family traumas, homelessness, sexual abuse, date rape, pregnancies, eating disorders, and so on.

Pam and Richard briefly discuss the other small crises that occurred that day at the school. Then Richard slowly pushes himself away from the wall and starts to walk away. He pauses, turns back toward Pam and says, "I swear, when I first began working as a counselor, I worked with only one crisis a month. Now it seems like every hour I have a crisis. It can be anything—sexual harassment, drug problems, guns on the school grounds, or suicide. My job has really changed over the years—but what's worse, all too often this school is the only home some of these kids have!"

CHANGING STUDENT NEEDS AND THE TEACHER'S ROLE

Teachers want answers. We know the needs of today's students are changing. We know we face more intense challenges with students today than teachers did thirty years ago. We are all too familiar with the difficult situations our students cope with daily. We know they come to school ill-prepared to learn because of problems they are facing at home or in their communities. Physical and emotional abuse or neglect, parental mental illness, alcoholism, drug addiction, criminal behavior, parental indifference—we know the problems, and we are all too familiar with our feelings of hopelessness and powerlessness in response. We watch our students starting out on pathways to self-destruction and feel helpless. Frustrated, disheartened, and feeling ineffectual, we have thoughts of leaving the career we dreamed of. We need answers. We need to know effective ways to deal with the complicated human situations we encounter daily in our classrooms—and we do not want to be social workers. We are teachers!

The Answers in This Little Book

This little book describes effective, role-appropriate ways for teachers to make a difference for our students. It defines ways we can help the growing number of our students who live in high-risk situations—without becoming social workers *or* adding more work to our already busy schedules. Drawing from a qualitative study (Deiro, 1994), I describe the behavior of actual teachers—what they did that made a difference for their students. For some of us, these teaching exemplars will affirm things we are already doing. If this is true for you, I hope you are reassured and encouraged by research that supports the importance of what you are doing. You *are* making a difference for your students. For others, these teaching exemplars and corresponding data provide valuable ideas and insights into how we can become more positive influences in the lives of our students. This book illustrates ways to help students without assuming additional committee work or adding more responsibilities to our overloaded schedules. The behaviors illustrated are intrinsic to our jobs as teachers. In essence, the teaching exemplars and corresponding data highlight ways we can simultaneously improve our teaching skills and help our at-risk students.

The Key to Making a Difference

The most powerful and effective way teachers can help students overcome the negative influences in their environment is by developing close and caring connections with them (Benard, 1991; Brook, Brook, Gordon, Whiteman, & Cohen, 1990; Deiro, 1994; Hawkins, Catalano, & Miller, 1992). In fact, the healthy development of children in today's society is *dependent* on having more caring adults meaningfully involved in their lives. Richard, in the opening story, is right. Today's students *are* different. Their social and emotional needs are not being met the same way those needs were met several generations ago. Young people today do not have enough adults in their lives who know who they are and genuinely care about them—a prerequisite for healthy emotional and social development. This shortage of caring adults makes a meaningful, caring teacher-student connection even more essential than in past generations.

This chapter begins the discussion about the power of healthy teacher-student connections. First, it documents the positive impact healthy relationships with caring adults have on a young person's social and emotional development. More specifically, it includes descriptions of several studies that document the impact of caring relationships with teachers. The chapter ends with a conceptual model for defining a healthy, caring teacher-student relationship, leading us into the next chapter where we explore ways to make those healthy connections without adding responsibilities to our job.

HEALTHY CONNECTIONS EQUAL HEALTHY DEVELOPMENT

Strong, healthy connections with prosocial adults have been identified as the key protective factor buffering children against the negative influence of adversity (Benard, 1991; Brook et al., 1990; Hawkins et al., 1992). Prosocial adults are individuals who obey the laws of society, respect our social norms, and care about the well-being of others. For example, being strongly connected with a parent who smokes marijuana, or who drives drunk, does not foster healthy social and emotional development. Being strongly connected with a parent who models good work habits, shows respect for societal laws, and is actively concerned about the well-being of others *does* promote healthy development. It does not matter what the adversity is (e.g., living in poverty or a high-crime area, parental indifference, social isolation, or parental abuse), having a positive connection with at least one prosocial adult mediates the negative impact of adverse situations. Children value adults who value them. Thus children who are living in seemingly intolerable situations but have a prosocial adult outside their home environment who cares about them will adjust their behavior to carefully safeguard that relationship. In doing so, the child begins to internalize the prosocial value system of the caring adult. For these reasons, strong, healthy connections with prosocial adults are essential to a child's healthy social and emotional development (Bowlby, 1988; Bronfenbrenner, 1986; Brook et al., 1990; Glenn, 1996). Without caring relationships with prosocial adults, the prospects of a healthy social and emotional development are markedly diminished.

What Happened?

Today, there are too few prosocial adults actively involved in the lives of our children. Since 1940, American society has undergone tremendous changes in demography, economic structure, and lifestyle. These changes have reduced the number of adults readily available to be involved in the lives of young people. To begin with, until the 1930s the United States was primarily a nation of people who lived on farms or in small communities. By the 1950s this census statistic had changed significantly. Due to a combination of factors such as the baby boom, easy mobility, and postwar job opportunities in cities, the United States has become a nation of people who live primarily in large cities or suburbs. This major demographic shift in such a short time brought with it many cultural changes, and we did not fully comprehend the impact of those cultural changes on the social and emotional development of children. With the migration to the cities, young families lost the nurturing support of large extended families, lifelong friends, and close neighbors. They lost the familiarity that naturally comes when living in small or rural communities. In short, our children lost their network of caring adults who know them well, watch them grow up, and even help with their parenting. No longer can a child expect to have a grandma or an Aunt Sue nearby to offer hugs and reassurance during difficult family times. No longer is there an Uncle George or lifelong friend available to attend a child's school play when Mom has to work, or Dad is drunk. Other demographic changes within the family, such as the increased number of women who work outside the home and the increased number of single-parent families, have even further reduced the number of caring adults and amount of time they can spend with their children.

Education's Response to Societal Shifts

The demographic trends of the 1940s and 1950s also brought changes to our educational institutions that further decreased the number of caring adults meaningfully involved in the lives of young people. The baby boom of the 1950s brought with it large, consolidated schools. Census statistics show the number of high schools stayed relatively the same from 1930 to 1970, despite the population boom (Coleman, 1974). Schools were reorganized from small schools in small districts to large, consolidated schools in large districts. Classroom size shot up from an average of twenty students per classroom to an average of thirty-six students per classroom (Glenn, 1989). Larger classrooms meant fewer teachers for more students. More students per teacher meant fewer opportunities for students and teachers to make individual contact or engage in conversations. These conditions decreased the opportunities for teachers to make quality connections with students and further reduced the number of adults with whom young people could develop close and trusting relationships.

Technology Further Complicates the Problem

Advances in technology have also contributed to the decrease in the quality of connections between adults and children. Technological advances such as the television, videocassette player, and the computer make life more pleasant, but they cut down on opportunities for meaningful interaction. Television is a passive, relaxing, low-concentration activity. The average American spends four to six hours a day watching television. Twenty-five percent of all time spent at home with family members is spent watching television, not talking to one another (Herr, 2001; Kubey & Csikszentmihalyi, 1990). Television is gradually replacing meaningful dialogue and quality time with adults. Some child development experts claim the influence of television on children today has surpassed the influence of church, family, and schools (Glenn, 1989). Our churches, families, and schools were once considered the shapers of our nation's children. Television producers and television characters now hold that power.

What Did We Lose?

Of course, the past was not perfect and all children did not live in caring families. But there were more opportunities for other caring adults to develop healthy connections with young people when communities were smaller, classrooms were smaller, and the media provided fewer distractions. Everyone knew their neighbors and their neighbors' kin.

Young people often spent time in the company of older, more mature members of the family or community, working side-by-side, which created an apprenticeship for adulthood. Communities took responsibility for raising a child. These intergenerational bonds are what is needed to facilitate the healthy emotional and social development of our children. In the past, caring connections automatically facilitated the healthy development of young people, something we as a nation did not realize—and took for granted. We did not realize that we have to do more than feed, clothe, shelter, and love a child for that child to develop into a healthy prosocial adult. It takes more than just a single family to support the healthy emotional and social development of a child. It takes several caring adults.

Today, our rapid-paced, geographically mobile lifestyle makes it very difficult for us to find quality time to spend with young people. Intergenerational bonds are difficult to form. And without time to form meaningful connections, prosocial adults do not and cannot automatically play a key role in shaping the emotional and social development of young people. We are now facing the consequences of not having an "apprenticeship for adulthood" for our children, and, painfully, we teachers see the repercussions played out in our classrooms and in our students' lives. Yes, today's students are different. Today's teachers *are* dealing with more student problems than yesterday's teachers had to face. Many of the problems we face in our classroom today result from the lack of caring adults meaningfully involved in the lives of children.

Working Toward a Solution

We cannot expect to return to a past when women stayed at home, the majority of Americans lived on farms or in small communities, and technology was the topic of science fiction. That is not going to happen. Present economic demands, personal desires, and technological advances preclude that lifestyle. We need to discover solutions compatible with our present-day lifestyle to increase the number of caring adults actively involved in our children's lives. Those of us who are regularly in touch with young people need to discover new ways to use the time we have with children wisely and constructively. We need to understand how to develop close and caring relationships with young people within limited time frames, with limited contacts, and with limited resources.

Teachers Play a Key Role

Parents, primary caregivers, extended family members, close friends, neighbors, community members, and youth leaders can all play important roles in rebuilding the network of caring adults surrounding young people. But of all the various professionals who have the potential to change young lives, probably none have greater potential than teachers.

We have the greatest access to the most children for the longest period of time—sometimes even more than parents or primary caregivers. We are in touch with young people six hours a day for nine months of the year. For this reason, we can be a rich resource for rebuilding the network of supportive, caring adults that young people so sorely need.

To really take advantage of being a rich resource for young people, we need to reassert and reemphasize one of our primary teaching responsibilities—the development of positive and meaningful connections with students (Glenn, 1989; Goodlad, 1990; Lieberman & Miller, 1984; Noddings, 1988, 1992). We need to bring this responsibility to the forefront of our nation's expectations for teachers and for teacher education curriculum. We need to discover and advocate for appropriate ways to become meaningfully involved in our students' lives. Educational administrators need to find ways to support and encourage teachers who are developing caring relationships with students. Community and national efforts to improve education need to make the development of caring school environments a priority. If this is done, teachers can truly become a significant cadre of caring adults in the lives of students. In turn, we teachers will enhance the healthy development of young people and make a difference.

Research Documenting the Power of Teachers

Research on bonding documents a powerful way we can make a positive change in our students' lives. Although few, there have been some studies that highlight the power that teachers have. For example, in a classic thirty-year longitudinal study of Hawaiian children living in adverse home conditions, Werner and Smith (1992) traced factors that helped these children grow up to be successful, well-adjusted adults. More often than not, the key factor was a caring, responsive teacher. Werner describes the children who navigated these discordant homes to successful adulthood as resilient, which means they had the ability to rebound or recover from adversities that could have caused serious psychological harm. These resilient adults raised in adverse home conditions frequently mentioned a favorite teacher as the person who really made the difference for them. In another classic study about the impact of adverse home conditions on children, Rutter (1987) concluded that children from disadvantaged and discordant homes are less likely to develop emotional problems if they attend schools that have caring, attentive personnel and good academic standards. The findings of these classic studies are now being corroborated by other researchers who discuss the teacher-student relationship as key to changing student attitudes and behavior (Hall, 2003; Hoffman & Levak, 2003).

In another interesting study, a caring, compassionate teacher had a positive long-term effect on a group of Holocaust survivors. Moskovitz (1983) studied twenty-four concentration camp survivors who were children when held captive by the Nazis. These individuals were sent to an orphanage in England at the end of World War II. In interviews with them thirty-seven years later, Moskovitz was amazed at the positive feelings they had about life. The survivors attributed these positive feelings to a teacher in their orphanage who provided them with warmth and caring and encouraged them to treat others with compassion.

Other studies also acknowledge the impact of one responsive, caring teacher on students. Pedersen, Faucher, and Eaton (1978) found that a caring, prosocial first grade teacher helped children from a disadvantaged urban neighborhood overcome adversity and become successful prosocial adults. O'Donnell, Hawkins, Catalano, Abbott, and Day (1995) found healthy connections to teachers were associated with a decrease in delinquency or behavioral problems, an increase in social and academic skills, and higher scores on a standardized achievement test. McLaughlin and Talbert (1990) found personal bonds with adults in the school have greater capacity to motivate and engage students academically than do the more traditional forms of social controls that emphasize obedience to authority or conforming to rules. These findings were later corroborated by other researchers who found student academic motivation increases when students have caring teachers (Dolezal, Welsh, Pressley, & Vincent, 2003; Erwin, 2003; Marzano & Marzano, 2003; Mendes, 2003; Wentzel, 1997; Wolk, 2003). These studies help document what we already intuitively know: a caring, responsive teacher has a positive influence on the overall development of young people.

MEETING STUDENTS' NEEDS: THE CARING TEACHER

In light of the above research—as well as what we know intuitively—there is little doubt that a positive connection with a caring teacher can make a real difference for students. Consequently, identifying effective and appropriate ways for us to help our students navigate childhood to successful adulthood may be as simple as knowing role-appropriate ways to develop close and caring connections with them. It sounds simple, yet when we set out to uncover possible appropriate ways to build these close and caring relationships with students, information is disturbingly scant. When we attempt to visualize role-appropriate ways teachers can develop caring connections with students, images are foggy. More often than not our images involve some type of hybrid of the role of a counselor or social worker. We see ourselves as being incredibly focused on the needs of each child, always available and willing to listen, responsive to all the needs of our students, patient and with endless time—hardly realistic when we consider the number of students we work with and our responsibilities as teachers. Making meaningful connections with students does require giving individually focused time, attention, and support to students. How can we possibly develop caring connections with 150 students a day without compromising our primary academic responsibilities? The task seems daunting. If we are to assume a more active role as caring adults in student lives, we need to discover realistic, reasonable, and time-effective ways to nurture connections that are compatible with our daily teaching responsibilities.

Appropriate Ways to Develop Close and Trusting Relationships

Understanding appropriate ways for teachers to develop caring relationships with students is contingent upon understanding the unique characteristics of a teacher-student relationship. We form our caring relationships with students for a distinct purpose that is very different from the reasons we form other social relationships.

Four Types of Social Relationships

Bennis, Schein, Steel, and Berlew (1968) have identified four types of social relationships based on the purpose for which they are formed: expressive-emotional, confirmatory, instrumental, and influential.

1. Expressive-Emotional
Expressive-emotional relationships are formed for the purpose of fulfilling ourselves. Friendships, romances, love, and marriage are examples of an expressive-emotional relationship. Usually when we are thinking or talking about relationships we have this type in mind. In fact, we are bombarded daily with references to the expressive-emotional relationship. Songs proclaim its virtues; books and films are created around the theme. But there are other types of social relationships that are formed for different purposes.

2. Confirmatory
Confirmatory relationships are formed to confirm or clarify our values, beliefs, or social realities. Acquaintances who attend the same church or belong to the same political party are examples of confirmatory relationships. These individuals confirm our beliefs or values because they hold the same ones. We may be very happy to see them at church, or at political meetings, and we may even chat with them informally, but we seldom engage in other social activities with them such as going to a movie or having them over for dinner.

3. Instrumental
Instrumental relationships are formed in order to achieve a task or goal. Colleagues, work-related relationships, collaborators on projects, or

committee members are examples of instrumental relationships. We may like who we work with and even have fun at work together, but what draws us together is the job, not the relationship.

4. Influential

Influential relationships are formed to create a change in one or both parties in the relationship. The teacher-student relationship is an example of an influential relationship, and so are parent-child, counselor-client, doctor-patient, and parole officer–parolee relationships. The unique characteristics of the influential relationship help prescribe appropriate ways for teachers to show caring to students.

Characteristics of an Influential Relationship

Influential relationships are distinguished from other social relationships by several characteristics (Bennis et al., 1968). First, the central concern of the relationship is *intended change, growth, or learning*. The primary interest of the change agent (e.g., a teacher or doctor) in an influential relationship is the modification of the situation, behaviors, or attitudes of the change target (e.g., a student or patient). Second, the change, growth, or learning found in influential relationships is *planned*, not spontaneous or accidental. Third, when the change has been achieved or internalized, or as much as possible completed, the relationship is *discontinued*. In a healthy influential relationship, the goal is termination (e.g., advancement, graduation, discharge, parole). Fourth, the distribution of power among the participants in an influential relationship is *asymmetrical*. The change agent holds more power than the change target. With this asymmetrical balance of power comes responsibility. The change agent is expected to give more, to know more, and to understand more than the change target. As a rule, students learn from teachers, clients from counselors, patients from doctors. In healthy influential relationships, the change agent wields this power carefully and respectfully. The emotional needs of the change target must take precedence over the needs of the change agent. So, in a teacher-student relationship, the emotional needs of the student take precedence over the needs of the teacher. In summary, the characteristics of healthy influential relationships are intentional promotion of growth and change, the fostering of independence through encouraging internalization of the growth or change, and a respectful use of the asymmetrical balance of power.

Guidelines for Caring Behavior
in Teacher-Student Relationships

Knowing the purpose for a relationship helps us identify and define what behaviors are nurturing within that relationship. The four types of relationships mentioned are governed by different norms and codes of behavior. What may be considered nurturing and appropriate behavior in one type of relationship may not be nurturing and appropriate in another. For instance, whispering sweet nothings in the ear of a spouse may be nurturing behavior, whereas whispering sweet nothings in the ear of a student may be grounds for a sexual harassment or sexual abuse suit. When defining what teacher behaviors *are* appropriate expressions of caring, the characteristics of a healthy influential relationship—intentional promotion of growth and change, empowerment of students through internalization of learning, and respectful use of power—help frame our definition. As such, caring behavior of a teacher can be defined as doing our jobs well by promoting the academic growth and independence of our students and, in that process, respectfully and ethically using the power that is inherent in our position as teachers.

Friendships With Students: An Ethical Dilemma

Because of the asymmetrical balance of power inherent in the teacher-student relationship, an ethical dilemma is introduced for teachers who attempt to develop caring connections with students by trying to be their "friend." Young teachers are particularly vulnerable here. Attempts to alter the purpose of the teacher-student relationship to be more in tune with an expressive-emotional relationship—a relationship formed for the purpose of friendship, romance, love, or marriage—are difficult, inappropriate, and may even be unethical. One needs to ask whose needs are being met. The asymmetrical nature of an influential relationship always defines the student as the more vulnerable member of the pair. Because of the vulnerability of the student, behaving in a teacher-student relationship as the teacher might in an expressive-emotional relationship is not only *not* nurturing, it is *not* ethical. For instance, we should not share confidential personal information with students for the purpose of developing intimacy, nor should we step away from our role and responsibilities as a teacher when interacting with students in order to gain their affection and approval. The motive for our friendliness is the key. We can be friendly with our students, but we can not be their friend.

When Is It Appropriate to be a Student's Friend?

We know the purpose of an influential relationship is to achieve a goal and then closure. But once terminated as an influential relationship, can the relationship be redefined to be more in line with an expressive-emotional relationship? There are many hazards involved in making such a change. Before such redefinition, the original purpose for forming an influential relationship should be explicitly completed. Such completion is usually signaled by a ritual, a process, or a formal activity such as promotion or graduation. Even then, some influential relationships are nearly impossible to redefine, and really are not appropriate for redefinition. For example, with parent-child relationships, throughout their lives children usually hold a special esteem for their parents. Even when children move into adulthood and their relationship with their parents takes on the characteristics of an expressive-emotional relationship, a parent still holds a place of honor and esteem in the adult child's eyes. The same is true for the teacher-student relationship. Even though students may mature and move into adulthood, their teachers continue to hold a place of honor and esteem in their eyes because of the important role the teachers once played in their growth and development. We need only to ask ourselves, "Can this student ever really see us as his or her equal?" Equality is the foundation for a true friendship.

Redefining a teacher-student relationship as a confirmatory (based on shared values) or instrumental (based on shared tasks) relationship is usually easier and less ethically sensitive than redefining it as an expressive-emotional relationship. Only when two individuals who were involved in an influential relationship are separated for a significant period of time—usually two or more years—and then meet again on an equal footing is the development of an expressive-emotional relationship ethically defensible. Even then, care must be taken that the relationship is on an equal footing. Usually, if a relationship started as an influential relationship, it is ethically safest to behave as if it is still an influential relationship—even though no learning is being consciously planned and produced. So, when is it appropriate to become friends with previous students? I say only after years of separation and only if we come together again on equal footing—and even then, proceed with caution.

CRITICAL ANSWERS AND MORE QUESTIONS

We now know that healthy relationships with prosocial adults are essential for a child's healthy prosocial development. Because teachers have a responsibility to build effective relationships with students, the positive connections we form can play a meaningful role in the healthy development of our students. Research demonstrates that the close and caring connections teachers make with students have a powerful effect on their social and emotional adjustment. Such connections do make a difference for many young people navigating adverse or discordant conditions. An appropriate way to form such positive, nurturing connections with students is framed and defined by the responsibilities of our jobs as teachers, and the respectful use of the power given to us by virtue of our positions.

Nonetheless, we still need a picture of how we can make healthy, caring connections with many students in a short period of time. Developing such relationships requires that an adult give individually focused time, attention, and support. So, then, how do we make caring, positive connections with a classroom of twenty-five to thirty-five students? What does a typical teacher's behavior look like? What skills and sensitivities are helpful? And how can we be confident that our students perceive our behavior as caring?

We also need to take care of ourselves in this process. How can we prevent becoming emotionally drained and burnt out? How do we take care of ourselves with so many students wanting to connect with us? If we do not address this concern, how can we assume a caring role with confidence and some assurance of success? The answers to all these questions emerged from a qualitative research study I designed to discover role-appropriate ways for teachers to connect with students (Deiro, 1994, 1996). Those answers are discussed in the remainder of this book.

Although the way students respond to a teacher's attempts to make caring connections is important, this book does not discuss the many student variables that moderate the effectiveness of our caring behavior. A student's degree of social and emotional neediness and vulnerability plays an unpredictable role in his or her receptiveness to our caring. Some students trust more easily than others. Because of the many possible student variables, students are silent partners in the teacher-student relationships examined in this book. The focus of this book is only on what teachers do to nurture healthy teacher-student relationships and how caring teachers care for themselves.

2

*Making Healthy
Connections
With Students*

Tom's voice becomes softer, and he speaks more slowly as he continues to answer the question I just asked him: What experiences influenced your decision to become a teacher? As I listen to his answer I feel a lump develop in my throat. I am holding back tears. I divert my eyes downward. I do not want to make eye contact with Tom for fear my sentimental reaction to his answer will interrupt his train of thought. His response to my question has touched my heart.

"All my lousy teachers . . . and one man by the name of Francis M___. He was my literature teacher when I was a sophomore and a junior. He knew I had a lot of problems, but he always believed I was a good person and could do good things. I credit him with my life, literally. Without his belief in me, I couldn't have stopped doing the things I was doing."

I glance up at Tom and say, "That's exactly what this study is about . . . teachers who make a difference in students' lives."

Tom's eyes are red and well up with tears. Unembarrassed, he gazes back at me. Tom continues, "Mr. M___ was sort of a geek. He was the stereotype of an intellectual—horned-rimmed glasses, short, the works. Some students made fun of him, but we all knew he cared. The other teachers did not help me at all. They all knew I was having problems, but they didn't seem to care or believe that I could be different."

Tom pauses, glances away uncomfortably, and then looks directly at me and confidently says, "Even though I was doing some really outrageous things, and some I definitely shouldn't have been involved in, Mr. M____ still somehow could see through all the dirt and recognize that there was a good person inside. Mr. M____ believed in me."

Tom had been using drugs and even selling to his classmates. In the first week of his senior year, he was forced to drop out of school. The day he dropped out of school, Tom was required to fill out a form identifying what he planned to do in the future. All his teachers had to sign this form. Never fully comprehending why, Tom belligerently indicated he was going to become a teacher. "They all laughed . . . except Mr. M____. He actually told me he believed in me. He said he knew I would do what I said I would. I knew I could teach better than most of the teachers I had. And I know teachers make a difference in a child's life because Mr. M____ made a difference in my life."

WHAT WE DO TO MAKE A DIFFERENCE

We *do* make a difference for our students. On some level, we may all know this is true. What we may be unsure of is *what we do* that makes the difference. We now know that our influence on students resides in the quality of our *connection* with them. So how do we create those quality connections that make the difference? Many of us have personal impressions or beliefs about behaviors that nurture healthy connections with students. Naturally, these impressions color our thoughts on the topic. Some of us may think caring connections are made by being motherly—warm, empathetic, and gentle. Others may think we need to touch students, or be sweet, or permissive. While observing six caring secondary school teachers, I discovered something that seems to cut across all these personal impressions. I hope the information I discovered will offer us all greater direction and clarity in our attempts to make healthy connections with students.

A LITTLE ABOUT THE STUDY

In order to uncover what teachers do to nurture healthy connections with students, I used a qualitative case study approach. I sat in the back of the classrooms of six carefully selected secondary school teachers and observed what they did when they were teaching. The six teachers I observed were identified by their peers and supervisors as teachers who had solid reputations for developing strong, caring relationships with students in role-appropriate ways and who also exemplified excellent teaching overall. To verify that the teachers chosen truly did develop positive, healthy connections with their students, I had all their students take an inventory measuring how close and trusting they felt toward their teacher. A copy of this inventory is found in Chapter 3 (see Figure 3.1, Student Inventory on p. 55). Please feel free to copy it to use with your students.

I chose to observe secondary school teachers because they are faced with the greatest environmental obstacles when attempting to develop healthy relationships with students. Unlike elementary or postsecondary school teachers, secondary school teachers' work days are usually scheduled around fifty-minute segments of time with twenty-five to thirty-five students. These work restrictions leave the teacher little time to give individual students the attention and support necessary for nurturing a caring connection. I wanted to know how these teachers did it, thinking that if they can do it, surely all grade levels of teachers can do it.

I collected data on the teachers' behavior several different ways. I quietly observed each teacher in the classroom for at least three full days. (I did not observe them during extracurricular activities.) In addition to observing them, I interviewed each teacher four times for ninety minutes each time. These interviews were transcribed word-for-word, along with one ninety-minute interview with two students from each teacher's class. These students were randomly selected. I also informally talked to students. No complicated statistical analysis was done. In fact, the only statistics found in the study identify the percentage of students on free lunches, from special populations, or who chose to go to college. The data excerpts in this book and the vignettes at the beginning of each chapter come from the interviews with the teachers, the interviews with their students, or my observation notes.

MEET THE TEACHERS

I purposely selected six teachers who worked in three distinctly different socioeconomic school districts: inner-city, rural, and suburban settings. Two teachers from each school were observed—a male and a female. The teachers were from diverse ethnic backgrounds. They taught only traditional academic subjects: math, science, literature, and health. I wanted to observe teachers who taught only academic subjects because I knew that academic subjects present greater barriers to making individual connections with students than nonacademic courses such as shop or driver's education. The six teachers selected were not superstar teachers; they were singular individuals who were dedicated and motivated to help young people. They were like you and me. A brief description of each teacher can be found in Figure 2.1. You might want to mark this figure or copy it because it is easier to follow along with the different descriptive exemplars presented if you are aware of the unique characteristics of each teacher.

Teachers From Inner City High School

Dean. A thirty-eight-year-old Lebanese American male, Dean had been teaching ninth-grade biology at Inner City High School since the beginning

Figure 2.1   Meet the Teachers

INNER CITY HIGH SCHOOL	
DEAN	GAIL
• Ninth-grade biology teacher • Past college football player • PBS Golden Apple Teacher's Award • Easygoing disciplinarian • Taught for 6 years • Lebanese American	• Ninth- and tenth-grade language arts teacher • Poised and sophisticated • Tough as nails • Spends free time with students • Strict disciplinarian • Taught for 12 years • African American
RURAL CITY HIGH SCHOOL	
DALE	RUBY
• Ninth- and tenth-grade math teacher • Good natured and a natural athlete • Varsity boys' baseball coach • Easygoing but firm disciplinarian • Taught for 14 years • European American	• Ninth-grade health teacher • Committed to personal growth • Raised in abusive and unstable home • Soft-spoken but firm disciplinarian • Taught for 16 years • European American
SUBURB JUNIOR HIGH SCHOOL	
TOM	PAM
• Seventh- and eighth-grade social studies teacher • High school dropout • Experienced teaching both special education and highly capable students • Strict disciplinarian • Taught for 14 years • Italian American	• Seventh-grade social studies teacher • Successful businesswoman for 14 years prior to career change • Varsity girls' basketball coach • Strict disciplinarian • Taught for 6 months • European American

of his teaching career seven years ago. Before teaching, Dean worked as a chemist for five years in private industry. He returned to school at the age of thirty-one to become a teacher. Dean had won the Public Broadcasting System's "Golden Apple Award" for being one of six outstanding teachers in the state.

Dean readily admitted he was an easygoing disciplinarian. He felt this approach was best when working with inner-city students. Sometimes his classes had as many as thirty-six students. Incredibly full of energy, Dean always seemed on the move. When younger, Dean was a college football player; he was husky, with a charismatic personality and a remarkable devotion to and love for kids. Dean was assistant football coach and junior class advisor.

Gail. A thirty-six-year-old African American female, Gail had been teaching language arts at Inner City High School to freshmen and sophomores for only one year. But in total, Gail had twelve years of teaching experience at both the junior and senior high levels. She was a firm disciplinarian with high expectations of her students. Her counterpart, Dean, called her "Iron Woman" and said, "She is as tough as nails." Gail provided strict moral guidance with a compassionate and empathetic heart. Stylishly dressed, Gail was poised and sophisticated. She moved gracefully about the classroom.

Gail provided a culturally relevant curriculum for students of color, who made up 77% of the Inner City High School population. She was the drama club advisor and the advisor to the cheerleaders. She recognized her influence on her students' lives and used that influence to try to make their lives better.

Teachers From Rural City High School

Dale. A thirty-seven-year-old European American male, Dale had been teaching mathematics in Rural City since the beginning of his teaching career fourteen years ago. For the first four years of his career, Dale taught at Rural City Middle School. Then he moved to the high school to teach mathematics. Dale usually taught the advanced mathematics courses, but the year I observed him, he was teaching Fundamentals of Mathematics to freshmen and sophomores. About 20% of his students were mainstreamed students with special needs. Dale taught Fundamentals of Mathematics to see if he could help increase this special population's mathematics achievement scores on the standardized tests.

Dale readily admitted he was an easygoing disciplinarian. Of average height and weight, and a natural athlete, Dale moved quickly around the classroom. He was seldom seated. Once a college baseball player, Dale was the varsity baseball coach. For many years he also coached varsity basketball. Dale had a powerful commitment to helping kids be successful in their lives, and he consciously used his teaching and coaching skills to achieve that goal.

Ruby. A thirty-eight-year-old European American female, Ruby had been teaching health and physical education at Rural City High School since the beginning of her teaching career sixteen years ago. For the last six years she had been teaching only health classes, primarily to freshmen and sophomores. Ruby was a firm but soft-spoken disciplinarian. Physically fit and with a quick smile, Ruby conveyed a gentle and steadfast persona. She was the girls' varsity volleyball coach and assistant track coach.

Ruby was committed to the personal growth of her students and her own personal growth. She had a deep, abiding love and concern for children. Her own childhood was abusive and unstable. She was moved back and forth among her mother, her maternal grandmother, and foster home caregivers. Both her mother and grandmother had drinking problems. Ruby never knew her father. From these experiences, Ruby knew how important it was to be available for students and provide a stable, caring role model.

Teachers From Suburb Junior High School

Tom. A thirty-seven-year-old Italian American male, Tom had been teaching for fourteen years. For the past six years he had been teaching social studies at Suburb Junior High School. Tom had the educational training to teach both highly capable and special education students. Previously he had taught in alternative schools, special education programs, and accelerated programs. Tom was a firm disciplinarian with high expectations of his students. He supervised afterschool detention weekly and sponsored annual field trips to Washington, DC. A social activist, Tom approached his job with intensity and heart, yet he did not lose his sense of humor. He was actively involved in the governance of his school and in the promotion of school renewal programs such as interdisciplinary teaching and teaching to multiple intelligences.

Tom had been a rebellious teenager. He had used drugs throughout his high school years, dropping out of school his senior year. Tom knew what it felt like to be on the outside looking in. Tom dressed in a pressed shirt and tie for work. He was clean shaven with a short, crisp hair cut. Bright, creative, funny, and extremely dedicated, Tom believed in his students and nurtured their capabilities.

Pam. A thirty-nine-year-old European American female, Pam had been teaching social studies for six months at Suburb Junior High School. This was Pam's first year teaching. For fourteen years prior to returning to school to become a teacher, Pam had been a successful businesswoman in a glass-manufacturing company. In midlife, she made a change in careers in order to be of service to people, a core value for her. Working in the business world, she did not feel she was honoring this core value. As a teacher, she still had a matter-of-fact businesslike persona, although she dressed casually and moved sprightly among the students.

Pam was a strict disciplinarian with high expectations of her students. She coached varsity girls' basketball and chaired "Cool Cats," a team of teachers who were responsible for providing special attention and services to troubled students. Because Pam's childhood was abusive and difficult, she understood the impact of words on a young person's spirit and she was particularly aware of the needs of troubled students. Pam had made the transition from businesswoman to teacher well, taking with her important communication and negotiating skills learned in the business world.

Her innate brightness, genuineness, and love for children helped to make her an excellent teacher.

WAYS TO MAKE HEALTHY CONNECTIONS WITH STUDENTS

Seeing how these teachers made meaningful connections vividly illustrates how to make healthy, positive connections with a classroom full of students in just fifty minutes. From my observations and interviews, I identified several different strategies for making connections. Each teacher seemed to use a combination of at least two of these strategies consistently, and some teachers combined more. The strategies were

1. Creating one-to-one time with students

2. Using appropriate self-disclosure

3. Having high expectations of students while conveying a belief in their capabilities

4. Networking with parents, family members, and friends of students

5. Building a sense of community among students within the classroom

6. Using rituals and traditions within the classroom

The strategies outlined are assumed to be how these teachers made healthy connections with their students. There is no way I can really prove beyond a shadow of a doubt that the behaviors identified actually created the bond. However, what I do know for sure is (a) there was a positive connection between these teachers and their students, as evidenced by the inventories students completed, and (b) these behaviors are reported in the literature as essential to developing feelings of closeness and trust among individuals.

The descriptive exemplars presented are exact accounts of what I observed and illustrate how teachers can enact the strategy. These descriptive accounts give us an image of the behaviors, the skills, and the sensitivities helpful in developing close and caring connections with students. As I describe and illustrate these strategies, I hope you see something you already do or could easily incorporate into your teaching style.

CREATING ONE-TO-ONE TIME WITH STUDENTS

Psychologists have long suggested that when individuals spend time together while engaged in a caring and responsive dialogue, a bond develops between those individuals. Familiarity and trust form the basis for a healthy connection. The more time one spends with another, the more one has the opportunity to know and trust the other. The more positive experiences individuals share in a caring atmosphere, the more likely a healthy, positive connection is to develop. This perspective suggests that the more time a teacher spends with a student showing concern and caring, the more that student will develop feelings of closeness and trust with the teacher. With more than 140 students, though, sharing one-to-one time with each student seems like an impossible task for a teacher, especially a secondary school teacher. Yet *all* six teachers used some variation of this strategy to make their healthy connections with students. Some of the styles for creating one-to-one time were the same among all the teachers, and some styles were unique to a teacher. Here is how they did it.

Common Styles for Creating One-to-One Time

Some ways for creating one-to-one time with students were employed by all the teachers. For instance, they all made themselves accessible to students before class, between classes, and after school. They came to school early to open their classrooms so interested students could gather there and talk. When the bell rang between classes, they all stationed themselves at the doorway so that they could be accessible to students leaving and entering the classroom. They reached out to high-five or clasp hands with the students reaching for them. All these teachers remained after school with their classroom doors open, inviting students to come in and visit. They remained focused on students throughout the day. Tom says,

> As I walk to lunch or somewhere else, I could be focused on where I have to get and what I'm going to do, and *not* say hello or anything to any of the kids. But I stay alert especially in junior high because they are so social. I mean, if you walk by and don't say anything they take that as an insult.

Encouraging Personal Conversations

All six teachers gave freely of their time for personal dialogue with students as a way of making one-to-one connections. They were open for conversations with students about *any* topic, inviting students to talk freely with them. They knew that trust and rapport is developed when we hold in confidence personal information about another person (Johnson, 1972; Rogers & Webb, 1991). And they built trust and credibility by keeping confidential what students shared with them. These teachers had learned not to take responsibility for solving student problems but rather just to be good listeners, be supportive, and make referrals whenever possible. They knew how important it was for students to feel free to talk about whatever they wanted to share, and thus encouraged one-to-one conversations with students. They intuitively understood the psychological dynamic that if they learned something personal about each of their students they would not need to connect with 150 students every day. On days when they were not able to connect with a student, that student would still feel close to the teacher because he or she knew the teacher knew something personal about him or her.

Ruby, the ninth-grade health teacher, said she recognized that other teachers might not feel comfortable having students talk to them about personal things, but she explained that her desire to let students talk about anything goes back to her own educational experience. She said,

> A couple of my teachers really helped me out when I was really going through tough times. And if they had put walls up and said "I can't talk to you about this . . . this has nothing to do with class," or "I don't want to talk to you about this," that could have really affected how I turned out.

From vivid personal experiences, Ruby knew how important it was to remain open to whatever topics students brought up. She listened to students and then made the appropriate referrals. She did not pretend to be a counselor.

Like Ruby, Dale, the math teacher at Rural High School, valued being open to and knowing something personal about his students. He said,

> I say more than just "How ya doing?" I ask, "What's going on? What are you going to do this weekend?" I find out a little bit about each kid—where they live, what they're doing, what they like to do after school. Sometimes I ask them just to talk. And one time I asked that of a kid, and I found out that he flies airplanes. A fifteen-year-old kid who's up flying airplanes! And I thought "that's really cool!" because my dad was a pilot. And I thought you would never know that if you just get them in class and get them out. Each of these kids has a life that—some are good. They do great things. And some are really harsh. And I figure if I can get one of the harsh kids to maybe open up just a little bit and just get something out they'll feel better. Not to use it against him, not to do anything, just to show him that one person might care.

Encouraging Conversations During Nonclass Times Only

Some of the observed teachers allowed such personal dialogues with students only during nonclass time, that is, between classes, before and after school, or at school events. Using personal dialogue this way, the teacher retains the classroom as a quiet academic environment. There is little social interaction between teacher and student during class time. Between classes, though, and before and after school, the classroom becomes a hub for playful interaction and meaningful dialogue between teacher and student.

Gail provides an example of a teacher who used direct personal dialogue only during nonclass time to create one-to-one time with students. She taught language arts, primarily to freshmen, at Inner City High School. She had high expectations of her students and strictly enforced the rules of conduct in her classroom. There was a respectful silence in her classroom when students were working independently. But during nonclass times, Gail playfully interacted with her students. She talked to them about their personal problems or things that happened to them the previous evening. Students gathered in Gail's room before and after school and between classes, and not just to talk to Gail. Sometimes they came to talk to each other. Gail would join in the fun. She interacted with her students much like a mother or big sister would, telling them what to do and how to straighten out their act. One morning before school, Gail was sweeping the floor, getting ready for the day to begin. She was chatting with a student, Susan. They were bantering back and forth. Gail was quizzing Susan about her new boyfriend. Apparently Susan's boyfriend got caught carrying a weapon and fighting at a school game the night before. "Is he a smart student?" Gail quizzed. "Uh huh!" Susan responded. Gail quipped, "That is what you said about the last one." Gail continued razzing the student more about her choice of boyfriends, asking more questions about the relationship. When the bell rang and the students started to take their seats, she quietly said to Susan, "Don't stay with this one."

Gail claimed that she made personal connections with students by "being nosey." Once, during our interview session, a student interrupted our conversation. She turned her attention fully on him. After responding to his concerns, she directly asked him a question about his personal life. Afterwards she turned back to me and said, "See, I'm nosey. That's why I know everything going on in everybody's life." When her students were asked how their teacher learned about them, one student said, "She just asks people. She talks to everybody. She's got a way of staying aware of her students and how they're . . . if they're screwing up or not." Another student said, "Just talking to her. You know, I talk to her and she asks me about my family."

Openness to Conversations

All six teachers were recognized by their students for their openness to conversations with the students and interest in their students' personal lives. A student said of Ruby, "You can really talk to her . . . you can talk to her and that's the teacher who cares—that will communicate with the students." Students knew they could have their teacher's time if only they asked for it. And students recognized the importance of their teacher's interest in their personal lives. When giving advice on how to be a caring teacher, one student said, "Just take a little extra time out to care because there's a lot of things going on with a lot of the students these days—like parents or boyfriends. Just take some time out to understand that everyone has problems and just might be having a bad day."

Getting Involved in Extracurricular Activities

In the interviews, each teacher identified extracurricular activities as a key way to create more one-to-one time with students. Therefore they extended themselves beyond the classroom in a variety of school-sponsored activities such as coaching, field trips, student clubs, or sporting events.

In summary, these general techniques, such as making oneself accessible to students, giving freely of one's time for individual conversations with students about anything, getting involved in extracurricular activities, and staying focused on students when walking the halls, were used by all the observed teachers in their efforts to create one-to-one time with students.

Distinct Styles for Creating One-to-One Time

In addition to the common techniques for creating one-to-one time, several teachers had distinct styles. I observed four distinct styles: (1) designing curriculum to maximize individual or small-group contact, (2) interspersing personal and academic talking, (3) providing personally written comments on papers, and (4) using nonverbal communication such as touching and standing close to students. Some of these distinct styles can be replicated by any of us who teach. Others may be more difficult for us to replicate because they are unique to the teacher's personality.

Designing Curriculum to Maximize
Individual or Small-Group Contact

One way for creating one-to-one time with students when there are twenty-five or thirty students in a classroom is to design curriculum so students can work on projects in small groups of three or four. The teacher then interacts with these small groups, giving individual attention to each group. Students within the group feel a personal connection. With only six or eight groups to interact with, we are better able to focus attention and engage in meaningful dialogue with a group or particular members of a group. When one member of the small group is addressed, all members tend to feel involved in the conversation, especially when the conversation focuses on a project for which the entire small group is responsible.

Dean, the biology teacher at Inner City High School, provides an example of designing curriculum to create one-to-one time with students. He designed his curriculum to be small-group oriented, consisting primarily of experiential activities and exercises. His average classroom size was thirty-two students. He arranged his classroom so students worked in clusters of three, four, or five, creating about seven to ten small pods. He spent little class time lecturing. At the beginning of class, he briefly described and assigned a group activity. Then he raced around to all the groups responding to individual student concerns, interacting on a one-to-one basis or with the small group. When asked how he sees himself creating quality time with each student, he said this about working with small groups:

> You just gotta rush around and it's hard. You know something? You saw those classrooms. Second and fifth periods are less rowdy because there are less kids. I can get to more [students], and there are more [students] on task. Third and sixth periods I have a helluva lot of kids. There're thirty-five and thirty-six. That's too many kids in a science classroom . . . . friggin' ninth graders! Oh my gawd! Their hormones are crazy. They're just going crazy all the time.

When talking with a student in a group, he often squatted to bring himself eye-level with the student, or he placed his elbows on the table and braced himself on them, his body bent over so he was eye-to-eye with the student. Dean was able to remain focused on the students he was working with even though others were shouting at him and the classroom was noisy. He always used a soft voice. Dean's ability to remain intensely focused aided him in establishing personal contact.

Dean often left the last five to ten minutes of class for open time to socialize with students, teasing playfully or talking earnestly. This free time created more time for Dean to establish personal contact with his students, although this was not his primary reason for structuring his lesson plans in this way. Dean empathized with students' need to socialize. He believed social time helped to keep his students coming to class, a chronic concern at Inner City High School. He said,

> I never, ever forget what it was like when I sat in that seat. I never forget that the most important thing to me wasn't learning the life cycle. The most important thing to me was the social aspects of school, and if I can somehow incorporate those into a learning environment, then I'm going to be better off.

Interspersing Personal Talk During the Lecture

By interspersing personal talk during the lecture, students are informally and personally acknowledged intermittently during a traditional lecture or during other academic activities. The dialogue with a student may or may not concern the topic of the lecture or activity. Although these teacher-student connections may be brief, student quotes affirm how meaningful for them these brief connections are.

Dale provides the exemplar for interspersing personal and academic talk during the traditional lecture to create one-to-one time with students. He taught Fundamentals of Mathematics to freshmen and sophomores at Rural City High School, using primarily a traditional lecture mode with students seated in rows. He would take a few minutes to explain a mathematical concept on the blackboard. Then he would turn around, walk forward, and softly say something personal to a student or respond to a social question. After a moment of personal contact, Dale smoothly returned to his academic presentation without missing a beat. Dale did this or similar behavior many times during a class period. Here is what it looked like as described in my classroom observation notes:

> On the board, Dale works another problem. He stops, turns, and says to a female student, "New boots?" She answers, "No." Dale responds, "They were just shined?" She replies, "Yeah." Dale comments, "I need to get some new shoes." Other students pipe in about good types of shoes to buy. Dale listens, nods in acknowledgment, and then continues with his lecture as if it was never interrupted.

Another example from classroom observation notes:

> All of a sudden Dale says, "Did anyone see my picture in the paper last night?" Several students say "Yes!" Dale says with a big grin, "You guys pass!" He returns to his lecture and adds a few more points about math and then pauses again and says, "Jane, you got your hair cut." She smiles and nods. Another female student who had her hair in a ponytail says, "I got my hair cut but you didn't notice." Dale humbly replies, "You're right. I didn't notice." He returns to the lesson at hand.

Dale used this strategy throughout an entire class period, stopping his presentation every couple of minutes to connect. The class periods rolled by with the unique blending of academic lecture and social comments. Sometimes Dale would pause to say something personal to a student, and other times he would talk to students during the shuffling of papers when worksheets were being handed forward. Sometimes he would stop by a student's desk and ask how the new home was coming along. Other times he would stop to check with a quiet student, making sure he or she understood the material, while other students were working on problems.

Surprisingly, Dale was unaware he used this distinct style for creating one-to-one time. It came naturally to him. But even more surprising, Dale did not lose his original train of thought, even when interrupted by a social comment from a student. He simply responded sincerely and then returned to his original thought without losing a beat or even appearing flustered. And, I observed, the interruptions did not make the lecture seem disjointed or get out of hand. The process just appeared to be natural and flow easily. As an example, after showing the class a trick to use to learn percentages, Dale turned to face the class. A student interrupted by saying, "If I buy a new pair of cleat shoes, can I play baseball?" Dale answered, without missing a beat, "Anyone can play if you can hit, run, field, and throw. Can you hit?" "Yes." "Can you run?" "Sometimes." "Can you field?" "Yes." "Can you throw?" "Yes." "Three out of four . . . what percentage is that?" he asked the whole class. And they smoothly returned to the lesson on percentages.

Students were keenly aware of Dale's distinct style and even collaborated with it. Often they would interject a social question or comment for Dale before he could. Students commented on Dale's efforts to talk to everyone. Annette, a student, said,

> Every day he tries to make it a point to talk to every one of the students in his class, and he tells us that he tries to. All of a sudden he'll stop and he'll go, "Wait! You know, hi Annette. I haven't said hi to you today." Then he finishes what he was doing. So, I mean, that makes you feel good because that shows that he cares.

Danny, another student, endorsed Annette's comments by saying, "Well, he tries to talk to every person in the classroom every day. He'll ask, 'How're you doing?'" Danny then went on to say, "Almost everybody plays sports in [Dale's] class. He always asks them how their game went and who won. He knows something about what every person in the classroom does outside, which is nice. And he talks to everybody."

Using Written Comments

I observed two other unique techniques for creating one-to-one time: using written comments and nonverbal communication. These two techniques were used primarily to augment other strategies for making connections with students, rather than as a primary strategy for developing relationships with them.

Because Ruby's teaching style did not facilitate verbal connection with each student every day, she reached out to them through written comments and writing assignments. In her classes students did worksheets that were submitted at the end of the class period. Ruby often made personal comments on their worksheets. About creating one-to-one time with students, Ruby said,

> Sometimes it's really hard to get around to every student during a given class day. But I just try to make them feel wanted and noticed

and appreciated in here. They do lots of written assignments, so I'll write a lot of little things on them like, "good effort today," or "You had some great thoughts today," or "That must have been a rough experience to go through. I'd like to talk to you more about this." I'll try to put little personal messages to them.

Because students trusted Ruby to maintain confidentiality, they often used the written assignments to communicate personal thoughts to her. One student, Sally, said of Ruby, "I feel real comfortable writing down how I really feel and stuff. And like, if I have anything to hide from my family, I can write it down. Because I know she cares and she won't go around telling."

Ruby knew that many students who could not connect with her verbally could connect with her through their writing. She said, "Most kids are real willing to connect. If they cannot say something verbally, they're real willing to at least write it on paper." She goes on to emphasize, "I mean every conceivable thing that can happen to a kid has been written. So I feel that they know that I care and that I'm someone they can talk to in one way, shape, or form." For Ruby, student writing has become a powerful tool to establish personal contact in the classroom.

Using Nonverbal Communication

Nonverbal communication, such as direct eye contact, personal touch, standing next to a student, and nonverbal acknowledgments, can be ways to create one-to-one contact with students. Gail, Tom, and Ruby provide effective examples.

Gail's classroom nonverbally reflected her interest in her students and her efforts to establish personal contact. Remember, Gail was "Iron Woman." She ran her classroom like a tight ship where you could hear a pin drop, but she created a homey visual atmosphere in the classroom. She had a toddler picture of one of her students clipped to the front blackboard. She had four 2 ft. x 2.5 ft. framed picture albums resting on the chalk rail of her blackboard. They were filled with snapshots of students. Her walls were decorated with collages created by the students about themselves, sharing such things as their favorite foods, how they prefer to spend Saturday morning, current steady, favorite performers, and so on. These pictures reminded me of how a mother displays her child's work on the refrigerator. Students were treated like family members. Because Inner City High School student lockers had been removed from the halls of the school, many students had no place to leave their belongings. They used Gail's room for a "north wing" locker. Book bags lined the front wall of Gail's classroom. Gail acknowledged, "My room is sort of a locker room. I have certain drawers that certain students use. I have sweats and lunch kits and all kinds of things in those drawers."

Tom and Ruby provide examples of the use of touch to create one-to-one time with students. Their teaching styles were primarily traditional lectures with open discussions. This style limits the amount of personal, one-to-one time a teacher can spend with students. Tom and Ruby recognized the importance of one-to-one time for making positive connections but acknowledged the overwhelming difficulty of finding quality time to make those connections. Tom, a social studies teacher at Suburb Junior High School, said, "You have twenty-five to thirty kids in a class, fifty-five minutes. If you break it down per minute, that's maybe two minutes per kid. Not a whole lot of quality you can do in that time." Ruby said she tried to speak with every student but did not come anywhere close to it. Instead, she attempted to either stand by or walk by every student in her class during class time. She explained, "To be able to talk to every kid . . . there's just *no* way that's going to happen. You know, though, I can physically walk by them, and I do that much more so than I verbally acknowledge every single kid." Sometimes, when walking by a student, Ruby would touch his or her shoulder as a technique of acknowledgment. "I do get around the room a lot and I do human contact, put an arm on the shoulder, or whatever—safe contact—just to let them know that I appreciate their effort and just to let them know that I know that they're there. They're not just a face or a name or a number but they're a real human being."

Touch was also part of the way Tom made one-to-one contact with students. He strongly believed in appropriate touch with students. He said to me, "When you talk to my students one of the things they'll probably . . . I hope they mention, and if you watch me in class you'll see me go around and pat kids on the back, the kids who like to wrestle, the junior high age stuff. You know, that all has to be a part of it too because to them that's part of the contact."

Both Ruby and Tom were aware of the controversy around touching students in today's highly sensitive environment. They both acknowledged the need to limit touch, but also believed it was an important element in nurturing students. Ruby felt it was a little safer for female teachers to touch students than male teachers, but limited her touch to a student's shoulders. Tom believed there was big difference between a groping kind of hug and just a warm kind of hug that conveyed caring. He told his students at the beginning of the year that he was Italian and was raised with lots of touching and hugging. He let the kids know that he was going to touch and hug them. And he gave his students the option not to be touched. He asked students to tell him privately if touching was something they did not like and told them he would respect their boundaries, which he did. Tom considered touching too valuable to give up altogether.

Both male and female students came up to Tom and asked for a hug. Tom hugged the kids, teased them, and gently touched them on the head or shoulder when they were not feeling well. At one point in a lecture I observed, he reached out and touched a girl next to him. "Poor [student].

Figure 2.2

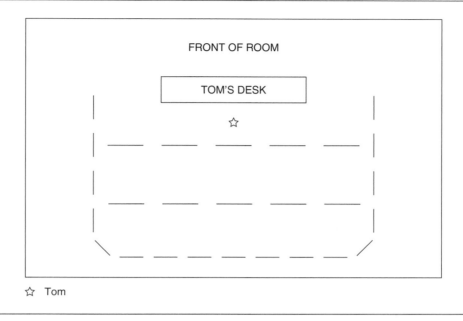

☆   Tom

You are not feeling very well. You are not giving me a bad time today."
Then he touched her on the head and gently rocked it. She weakly smiled
and the other students smiled also.

Eye contact was another nonverbal cue used to enhance contact with
students. Tom specifically arranged students' desks in his classroom in a
way that encouraged easy eye contact with each student (see Figure 2.2). This
arrangement also permits closer physical presence for the teacher when
lecturing or facilitating a group discussion. The desks are in a semicircle,
with two rows of desks dissecting the center of the semicircle. Tom taught
from the center of the semicircle sitting on his desk, or standing in front of
it, right in the midst of the students.

Summary of Ways to Create One-to-One Time

All six caring teachers had styles in common for creating one-to-
one time. They made themselves accessible to the students and remained
focused on student needs throughout the day. They were open to conversations with the students about any topic, inviting students to talk to them
and giving freely of their time for personal dialogue. In addition to the
styles in common for creating one-to-one time, several teachers had distinct approaches: (1) designing curriculum so that it maximizes individual
or small-group contact, (2) interspersing personal and academic talk, (3)
using written comments on student papers, and (4) employing nonverbal
communication such as touching and physical closeness.

USING APPROPRIATE SELF-DISCLOSURE

Johnson (1972), in his classic book on interpersonal effectiveness, discusses self-disclosure as the key to building a close personal relationship. "To like you, to be involved with you, to be your friend, I must know who you are" (p. 9). Without self-disclosure, truly close personal relationships are difficult to form (Johnson, 1972; Jourard, 1964). However, a teacher's role is to develop effective connections with students, not a close personal relationship. Students need to feel an emotional link to us and to trust that we will be attentive and responsive to their needs. A close, personal relationship with students though is not appropriate. But, when used appropriately, the strategy of self-disclosure can foster the development of healthy connections without creating inappropriate intimacy.

Self-disclosure appropriate for a teacher-student relationship is defined as the act of sharing or disclosing the teacher's own feelings, attitudes, and experiences with students in ways that are helpful to the students and enhance their learning process. When used appropriately, a teacher discloses information about himself or herself that is pertinent, in both content and context, to the needs of students. The personal information shared by a teacher facilitates learning. It also builds a bridge between teacher and student by connecting them on a common human level. Sometimes the self-disclosures provide examples to illustrate a concept the teacher is discussing. Sometimes the self-disclosures are used primarily to develop trust and build a close and caring connection. When used inappropriately, a teacher discloses information to satisfy the teacher's emotional needs to confess, cathart, grandstand, or manipulate.

Self-disclosure was a primary strategy that Tom and Pam used to develop healthy connections with their students. They provide superb examples of how teachers can use self-disclosure appropriately and effectively. Although both Tom and Pam employed this strategy, their individual styles give examples of several different ways to apply the strategy.

Pam's Style of Self-Disclosure

In her social studies class at Suburb Junior High School, Pam did a lot of teaching by analogy, using her personal experiences as examples. She told of her failings and mistakes as well as successes—if it served to emphasize and clarify a point. "I tell them things that aren't all that great sometimes [laughter] about myself . . . failings and mistakes and stuff like that, if I think it serves a purpose." Some of these self-disclosures about her failures were disarmingly honest and revealing. Pam shared stories about herself that could happen to anyone, but she did not share intimate, personal information. The self-disclosures she made were stories students could relate to and identify with. "I do a lot more self-disclosure than I think a lot of people do. But I am selective about what I talk about, too.

I almost never talk about my personal life, really, except some anecdotes that illustrate issues that come up." Pam also used analogous reasoning with her students and illustrated her thoughts with her own personal stories. She explained, "You know, [these stories] are not real self-revealing. They're kind of the 'everyman' kind of stories. I think they could happen to anybody. It could happen to any of my students."

Pam was clear that the purpose of self-disclosure was to enhance the learning process for students and to be genuinely and authentically human with students. She said,

> You know, the goal is to bridge the gap between us as people, but not become intimate . . . I want them to relate to me. I want to be able to relate to them. But I don't want to be on intimate terms with them. Nor do I want them to be on intimate terms with me.

Fortuitously, on one of the days I observed Pam, the seventh and eighth graders had an assembly on sexual and personal harassment. The assembly was forty-five minutes long, with four college students enacting eight to ten short vignettes depicting different types of harassment seventh and eighth graders deal with daily, such as poking fun at the way someone is dressed or looks, not selecting the geek to be on a baseball team, or teasing a female by snapping her bra by the back strap. The vignettes were poignant and sometimes even painful to watch. After the assembly, no time was allotted for students to discuss with an adult how they felt, what they learned, or what implications the lesson may have in their lives. Students were just dismissed to return to their normal class schedules.

As the students filed into Pam's classroom, their energy level was chaotic and their voices boisterous. Pam decided to set aside her prepared lesson plan in social studies and devote some class time to debriefing issues raised by the assembly. She began with a question. "How many thought the assembly was realistic?" Dead silence. No one ventured a response. Pam continued, "My stomach got tight during the vignettes. They brought up memories of painful experiences for me." Then she asked another question: "How many of us have been hurt by harassment, or have hurt others?" A few students slightly waved their hands, or quietly nodded their heads. Pam then told a vivid story about how, when she was in the seventh grade, she ridiculed a neighbor girl in an effort to gain the approval of a certain group of kids. She disclosed how embarrassed and ashamed she still feels about the incident. A couple of students began to talk then. They shared their own stories, talking about times when they harassed someone or when they were harassed. They talked about how they could do things differently. More students joined in. They talked about the possible reasons human beings are so mean to each other. They questioned the difference between flirting and sexual harassment. They discussed what they could realistically do if they were sexually harassed or caught up in peer pressure and harassing someone else.

Throughout the discussion, Pam skillfully interjected self-disclosures that kept the discussion focused, candid, and honest. For example, Pam did not let students give stock answers such as, "I would walk away" or "It doesn't bother me!" She recognized that students were trying to be tough or do the right thing. She did not reject these answers either. Instead, she talked about how she had tried similar behaviors, and how they had not worked for her. From her own experience, Pam shared how she had difficulty doing the right thing in similar situations. She shared how hard it was for her as a teacher to intervene in situations she overheard in the hallway. "Sometimes I am confused and don't know what would be best for me to do or what you guys would want me to do." Pam's self-disclosures created an hour-long valuable learning experience for what otherwise could have ended in a five-minute soliloquy.

At the end of the period, Pam's teaching assistant, an eighth grader, thanked Pam in front of the whole class for sharing a little of her own life with them. She said it was much easier to trust Pam and talk to her because Pam did share who she was with them. On this occasion, Pam skillfully and powerfully used self-disclosure to promote learning as well as connect with the students.

Tom's Style of Self-Disclosure

Tom also taught social studies at Suburb Junior High. Like Pam, he used self-disclosure to illustrate concepts he was discussing. But he also employed self-disclosure in another unique and effective way: he began each school year by creating an opportunity for students to get to know him personally. On the first day of class he did not hand out class rules and books or create his seating chart. He pulled up a stool and asked the students their names. On a sheet of paper he jotted down their names and began associating faces with names. Then he told them a few things about himself. He introduced the room to them, which contained not only historical items but other objects that gave students clues about who he was and the things that interested him.

For the final step in this process, Tom let the students ask him any question they wanted. He said he always started this question period by saying, "You know, I can walk down to the office and pull out your permanent record file and read all kinds of stuff about you, but you don't have the right to go down and ask for my permanent record file and read all kinds of stuff about me. So, this is your opportunity—what do you want to know?" During this questioning, Tom was careful to maintain his position of authority with the class, as is appropriate in an influential relationship. He said it was very interesting because usually students started out very tentative and very respectful when asking personal questions.

Invariably one of the questions that came up was, "I bet you were really a smart, good kid in school." Tom told them the truth—that was not who he had been. He told them about his father's death, about dropping out of school, about his past drug-dealing history, his shame in hurting people through his addiction. He told them every day he worked to make amends for the harm he had done to other people. Tom told them his story not because he was trying to be their friend or get them to like him. Tom knew he needed them to appreciate how he struggled as a young person because he was going to demand a lot of them academically and personally. He wanted to develop trust and rapport and the awareness that he could understand them and their struggles. Tom used self-disclosure primarily as a tool to begin bridging the gap between him and students by showing their common humanness.

Tom saw bridging the gap between him and students as key to success for the way he taught. He believed that if students saw a teacher as a human being who could make mistakes, they would believe that it was safe for them to make mistakes also. Tom knows that students work harder for teachers they like. And Noddings (1988) agrees. She says, "It is obvious that children will work harder and do things—even odd things like adding fractions—for people they love and trust" (p. 10).

Tom demonstrated one other interesting way for using self-disclosure as a teacher. When working with the troubled youth in the alternative school earlier in his career, Tom showed them his evaluation report. He explained, "When I was evaluated, after it was written up, I took it back to class, slapped it on the table, read it to them, explained to them what each part meant. They saw my report card!"

Tom was able to self-disclose this way and clearly maintain authority in his relationship with his students. Most of us do not have a history like Tom's, so this style of self-disclosure will not work for us. And for those of us who do have such a history, it is always risky to disclose past illegal or immoral indiscretions. It can backfire. But it is safe to disclose some past failings and struggles because they demonstrate our common humanity—and our acceptance and forgiveness of shortcomings in ourselves. This lets our students know that we will accept their shortcomings also.

HAVING HIGH EXPECTATIONS OF STUDENTS

A school culture of high expectations is a critical factor in increasing academic achievement (Hurn, 1985; McDermott, 1977; Noddings, 1988; Rist, 1970). Students from inner-city disadvantaged communities who choose to go on to college often attribute their motivation and success to having one person who believed they could do it (California Department of Education, 1990, as cited in Benard, 1991). The dynamic appears to be the internalization of high expectations by the students. Along with high expectations, when the message is consistently "You can do it. You are a bright and capable person!" one naturally sees himself or herself as bright and capable. Such a perception of oneself fosters a sense of purpose and gives hope for a meaningful future.

People like people who think highly of them, so it logically follows that students will like teachers who think highly of them. Students enjoy being around teachers who see them as bright and capable with bright futures in front of them. Therefore teachers who have high expectations of students while clearly conveying a belief in their capabilities will be more likely to develop positive connections with students. The key seems to be conveying a belief in student capabilities *along with* holding high expectations. This requires two distinct behaviors on our part. First, we have to establish and maintain high academic standards for the students. Second, we need to believe that students can meet these high standards. We convey a belief in students' ability to meet high standards by working from the assumption that students will accomplish whatever we expect of them. When there is evidence students are not meeting our expectations, we need to problem-solve from the perspective that something is blocking the student from utilizing his or her innate abilities. In this way, we communicate a belief in the student's ability even though he or she is struggling. In other words, we convey a belief in a student's capabilities by focusing on his or her academic strengths rather than expressing discouragement and disappointment about what the student is not able or willing to do.

Tom's Style of High Expectations of Students

Tom provides an example of high expectations while conveying a belief in students' capabilities. He said, "It doesn't matter what your socioeconomic class is, if you're going to lower your expectations you're being either racially, culturally, or economically bigoted." Tom pushed for excellence. "Your strategy should always be to set high expectations. People rise to your expectations. If you set them high, they'll go high. If you set them low, they'll go low."

Tom perceived students as capable, and students responded positively to that perception. Even with the special education students mainstreamed into his classes, he held high expectations and students responded. According to his student teacher,

> even the slowest . . . even with the groupings . . . I like the fact that [Tom] doesn't dummy down the curriculum. You see a lot of that when teachers make [student] groups up . . . this group works on different worksheets. But it's pretty much the same core material. He doesn't let them take advantage of their challenges. One kid Tom knows is having a problem, so he'll slow down, but he won't slow down so much that the kid is taking advantage of his

disability. The kid may still complain, "I can't do it that fast. Let's slow down some more." Tom just tells him, "You know, I'm going to slow down this far. You are capable of keeping up."

Students *were* able to keep up. Tom's educational background, with special training for working with both the special education and the highly capable students, may have given him the confidence to work with a diverse group of students, but all of us can learn from his example.

The clearest example of Tom's belief in the capabilities of all students came from an earlier experience he had teaching in an alternative school. Tom knew these kids had never read the classics. "We read *Treasure Island* together. When I got the book, you know, other teachers said, 'Well, those kids will never be able to read that!' I said, 'Yes. It'll take a while, but we'll get through it.' So we read *Treasure Island*." Once they completed the book, as a reward, Tom showed the students the movie *Treasure Island* and served them popcorn.

Tom had pretested these troubled young students at the beginning of the year. At the end of the year they showed two years' average growth in reading and three years' average growth in mathematics. Not one student had dropped out of the program that year. The year before, *every* student had dropped out of the program.

On one of the days I was observing Tom, he had students reading and analyzing Martin Luther King, Jr.'s speech on the philosophy of nonviolence. This speech has some complex ideas difficult even for adults to comprehend. Tom worked with the students, prodding them with questions, helping them understand concepts by relating the ideas to events common in their own lives: "How many of you would find it hard not to strike back at someone who is hitting you?" "Why do you think this non-violent approach works?" I could see students begin to understand the concept of nonviolence by the looks of disbelief and amazement on their faces. Tom did not talk as though he had all the answers, but as though he was exploring ideas right along with the students. Tom talked *with* the students, not *at* them or *for* them. Although he had high expectations, he showed respect. The learning atmosphere was safe. Students felt free to make mistakes without ridicule or embarrassment.

High Expectations for Teachers, Too

A critical component of conveying belief in our students' capabilities is for *us* to have high expectations of *ourselves* and our ability to teach. In this regard, we assume mutual responsibility for a student's confusion. This mutual responsibility conveys to students that a teacher believes students can understand when the message is clearly communicated. Tom held high expectations of himself and his teaching abilities. He realized that if students were having a difficult time learning, part of the responsibility rested with how *he* was teaching. Tom worked hard to create lesson plans that made concepts easy to grasp because they related to student experiences.

Tom's students recognized that both high expectations and hard work were mutual expectations. They appreciated Tom's shared efforts and hard work to promote their learning process. When questioned about Tom's style of teaching, one of his students, Jeremy, said proudly, "He makes sure you do your work. He makes sure that you have a passing grade." Students knew that Tom wanted them to work hard, to learn, and to pass the course, and that he worked to help that happen.

NETWORKING WITH FAMILY AND FRIENDS

Coleman (1985) describes a functional community as a community where "a child's friends and associates in school are sons and daughters of friends and associates of the child's parents" (p. 529). This two-generation loop is called an intergenerational closure. In schools situated in functional communities, parents know the parents of their children's friends, and teachers know the family, friends, and neighbors of their students. The intergenerational closure allows for a flow of information that strengthens and supports parents and teachers in school-related activities.

Making Connections With Family and Friends

Teachers who live and teach in functional communities have more opportunities for close relationships with their students. When we live in the same community as our students, we have additional opportunities for connecting with them outside the classroom. For instance, we may be friends with the child's parents, attend the same church as the child's family, or shop in the same grocery store. We have opportunities to make personal connections with the people who are important to our students. And the more important the person is to the student, the more helpful that connection is to us. These personal connections create a sense that the teacher is part of the family or community.

It is clear that we teachers can strengthen connections with students by living in the communities in which we work and becoming acquainted with students' parents, relatives, neighbors, and friends. Dale, mathematics instructor at Rural City High School, provides an example of networking with a student's circle of family and friends. Rural City High School is situated in a small rural community with a population of about 15,000. It is the only high school in the small, self-contained community. Self-contained communities are characterized by long-term residents, extended families living in the same area, neighbors familiar with neighbors, and business people and shopkeepers living in the communities in which they work (Coleman, 1985). Many of the local residents' families have lived and worked in Rural City for generations.

Dale has lived and taught in Rural City for fourteen years. The first four years he taught at Rural City Middle School; the next ten years he taught at Rural City High School. Dale believes it is important for teachers to reside in the community where they teach: "I've always felt that if you teach you should be a resident of where you teach. I've always felt that."

By actively participating in the community, Dale had many opportunities to meet his students' parents, family members, neighbors, and friends. Some students' older siblings or cousins had been his students in previous years. He had met parents and others through coaching his son's church-sponsored basketball team or through shopping. In the small community he saw students about town and met their parents and family members then. "You know, I go downtown and I know everybody almost, even though I wasn't a hometown boy—I wasn't born here." Some of Dale's personal friends were parents of his students. He said he often mixed socially with the parents of his students. His wife's best friend was the mother of one of his students. Some parents lived right down the street from Dale. Some students were in his neighborhood and came to his house to play basketball.

The extracurricular activities in which Dale participated also provided opportunities to get to know the parents. For instance, he took tickets for wrestling matches, volleyball, soccer, and football games. At the door he met the parents, family members, friends, and neighbors. "When you're at the door you know all the parents. You know who's there . . . they know me. So you build a little friendship that way." He was timekeeper for the girls' basketball games and coached varsity baseball, giving him additional opportunities to meet parents and other significant individuals in his students' lives. The personal and community connections Dale developed by living in the community created an intergenerational closure for students. Such closures provided a sense of community, with Dale part of that community. My observation notes demonstrate this sense of community and familiarity:

Before the next period starts, Dale and the students talk about the basketball game that sent them to the state basketball tournament. Several students ask where he sat at the game, and if he had seen their parents. He says, "Yes, I saw your parents." The students seem pleased.

Dale gives them a harder math problem to work and then walks around the class to help. He pats a male student on the back and says, "Does your mom want to talk to me yet?" The student smiles and says something back to Dale I cannot hear.

Dale is taking roll. A student pipes up and says it is her birthday tomorrow and she is having a party. Dale says, "We will all show up. I am sure Mike and Sue [parents of the student] will appreciate that." He continues to take roll. Dale is on first name basis with most of the parents.

In addition to providing a common circle of friends and acquaintances, intergenerational closures create additional sources of information about students. Teachers, as well as parents, gain other perspectives on a student's school-related activities. A child's needs and behaviors are less likely to remain unnoticed and unattended because there are added communication channels and multiple adults who are familiar with the child. For example, Annette, a student in recovery from alcoholism, said,

> He [Dale] knew that I had been doing bad in school but that now I'm trying and my grades are better and stuff. He's talked to my dad so he knows what my dad has told me about staying home [and working hard], and what to do if I've problems.

As evidenced by Annette's statement, the communication channel created by networking with her father provided an opportunity for Annette and her father to gain additional support, and Dale to gain additional information on Annette's situation.

Limitations on Opportunities for Making Connections

Opportunities for building healthy teacher-student relationships through networking with family and friends are not as available in less self-contained communities such as the suburbs. For instance, Suburb Junior High is situated in a typical residential bedroom community. The school is surrounded by a rapidly growing residential area, a recent product of the urban sprawl from a nearby large metropolitan area. Adults who reside there spend the majority of their day working or playing in other geographical locations. Few businesses are located within the jurisdiction of Suburb Junior High School. The community population is geographically mobile and constantly changing as families move into or out of the area. This shifting population and the lack of businesses in the community make it difficult for teachers to nurture connections with their students through networking with the students' circle of family and friends.

Bussing is another school practice that interferes with a teacher's ability to network with students' family and friends. Inner City High School was a perfect example of this conflicted situation. Thirty percent of the students who attended Inner City did not reside in the community surrounding the school. These students were bussed to Inner City High School from other communities. Also, some high school students residing in the community surrounding Inner City High School were bussed to other high schools. Even siblings or extended family members living in the surrounding community attended different schools than their brothers, sisters, or cousins did. Only 70% of the students attending Inner City High School resided in the surrounding community. Even though the community may have had many of the characteristics of a functional, self-contained community, the potency of networking with family and friends was diminished for teachers because of bussing.

Inner City High School teachers who chose to live and work in the community did have an opportunity, though limited, to become familiar with family and friends of some of their students, in spite of bussing. For example, Gail lived in the neighborhood of Inner City High School, and she recognized the value of living in the neighborhood as a means of building personal connections with students. She said, "This is my neighborhood. These kids live around me, and it's important for me to do well here because it's important for my neighborhood, very important . . . and because I live in the neighborhood." Sometimes Gail saw students while grocery shopping, getting gas, or walking the dog on the weekends or at night. While these informal meetings can help us make meaningful connections with our students, they also have their drawbacks. We lose our privacy and anonymity. We may not be able to run to the grocery store without taking special care that we are presentable because the checker is one of our students. But we can relish the fact that we get twice as much pepperoni on our pizza in restaurants where our students are the cooks! Knowing that we are developing healthy connections with our students and making a difference can be worth the added inconvenience.

BUILDING A SENSE OF COMMUNITY AMONG STUDENTS

Building a sense of community among students is another useful strategy for developing effective teacher-student relationships (Corey & Corey, 2002; Peck, 1987). Community, as used here, refers to a *relational* community where human interaction and social ties draw people together. Relational communities are defined as "networks of individuals who interact within formal organizations and institutions, and as members of informal groups" (Heller, 1989, p. 3). Common interests, histories, and experiences draw these individuals together and are the basis upon which social relationships develop (Heller, 1989).

In relational communities, a special cohesiveness develops among members. A genuine sense of community comes after the group members have committed themselves to taking significant risks and sharing meaningful experiences. In relational communities, group members become tolerant and accepting of each other. A feeling of belonging and relatedness develops among the members (Corey & Corey, 2002). These feelings of belonging and relatedness extend to everyone in the group, including the group leader and potential new members. According to Peck (1987), in genuine communities boundaries are soft. "[Members] do not ask, 'How can we justify taking this person in?' Instead the question is 'Is it at all justifiable to keep this person out?'" (p. 61). This group dynamic of genuine communities is called inclusivity. Inclusivity means there are no outcasts—everyone is welcomed.

Inclusivity may explain how building a sense of community among students may also enhance the teacher's connections with his or her students. As with other relational groups, when a teacher helps students develop relationships with each other by encouraging risk taking, honest self-disclosures, and sharing among class members, a sense of community develops among students. Students feel a sense of belonging and relatedness among themselves. With inclusivity, the teacher is drawn into the student community. Students feel connected to each other and connected to the teacher.

Ruby, health teacher at Rural City High School, provides an example of making healthy connections through building community among students. She designed her curriculum so that students shared personal values, attitudes, beliefs, strengths, and insights with each other on a regular basis. Through sharing, students got to know one another on a personal level. Ruby designed exercises and activities that created opportunities for her students to talk about things they valued, personal insights, or beliefs. She recognized that it is often difficult for students to reflect out loud, especially when they are asked to talk about their strengths, but she also knew how important it was for students to make appropriate self-disclosure. For example, Ruby had students put their first name in the middle of a 5 x 7 index card. Then she asked students to write the name of an animal they would be if they could be an animal. In the top left corner, students identified their favorite food, and in the top right corner, a safe place for them to be. In the bottom left corner, students named their favorite singer or movie or book, and in the bottom right corner, two positive qualities about themselves. Students then exchanged these cards with one another. Ruby always made a card for herself, which she exchanged with students she did not know very well. In another activity, Ruby asked the students to talk about something that made them angry and then an appropriate way to communicate that anger. During this activity, one student who was sitting in the back of the room was not engaging with anyone. Ruby gently approached her and asked, "Why don't you share with me?" The student hesitated and then started talking while Ruby patiently listened and responded with encouraging questions.

Ruby often asked students to write their ideas or thoughts down before sharing them. This made it easier for students to speak out loud. She also alerted students that they would be disclosing what they wrote to other students. She established ground rules that created a safe environment. When she noticed a student was having a difficult time sharing with another, she gently approached him or her, volunteered what she had written or volunteered to listen to the student. This encouraged all the students to participate.

Ruby worked hard to get students to open up and speak out loud about themselves in class. At the beginning or end of the week she saved time for talking about topics unrelated to the class material, as a technique to get students used to speaking up in class. They talked about movies, sporting events, and so on. Students were aware that they could talk about their feelings and important issues in Ruby's class and that this freedom to share helped them to feel close to Ruby.

> She has you write down your feelings a lot of times on stress and stuff . . . like about how you would cope with stress and your problems and . . . and she asks us how we'd solve it.

Ruby also encouraged students to bond to the larger school community, through involvement in extracurricular activities or supporting athletic events. She encouraged students to go to games, to get involved with school activities, and to develop school spirit. This additional bonding to the school increased the sense of community among the students and the sense of connectedness to the teachers.

PROVIDING RITUALS AND TRADITIONS

Throughout the ages, providing rituals and traditions has been a common strategy to bond individuals to their families, communities, institutions, or even country. Rituals are activities that are performed the same way each time they are introduced, such as every Friday having the last fifteen minutes of class reserved for open discussion, or beginning a social studies class with a current event introduced by a student. Traditions are customs, practices, or special events that are routinely acknowledged and honored, although how they are acknowledged and honored may be different each time. For instance, we may celebrate Martin Luther King, Jr. Day but create a different type of celebration each year in honor of the event.

Rituals and traditions help build a sense of community. They create a common experience for students, providing them with a common basis and a familiar routine. Ruby creatively used rituals in her efforts to build community among her students. For instance, at the beginning of her classes Ruby read, or had a student read, a "one minute message" from a daily inspirational reader. Ruby admitted she was not aware of how important this little ritual was until one day she forgot to do it. Students really complained. She then assigned a student to make sure the "one minute reading" was done even if she was not there.

As teachers, many of us are already using rituals or have traditions. We can easily come up with wonderful examples of rituals by simply reflecting on our teaching practice or by asking our colleagues to share some of the rituals they use. But knowing a particular ritual to use is not as important as recognizing that rituals and traditions help develop a sense of community in the classroom. We are *enhancing* our ability to develop close and meaningful connections with our students by using rituals and traditions.

SUMMARY OF THE WAYS TO CREATE HEALTHY CONNECTIONS WITH STUDENTS

The six strategies discussed in this chapter suggest appropriate ways for teachers to build close and trusting connections with students *without* compromising the primary responsibility of a teacher—academic achievement of students. The six strategies for making meaningful connections with students are

1. Creating one-to-one time with students

2. Using appropriate self-disclosure

3. Having high expectations of students while conveying a belief in their capabilities

4. Networking with parents, family members, friends, and neighbors of students

5. Building a sense of community among students within the classroom

6. Utilizing rituals and traditions in the classroom

These six strategies are probably not the only appropriate ways for us to develop meaningful positive connections with students, but they do illustrate simple and powerful ways to connect successfully with 150 students—without compromising student academic outcomes. By using these strategies, we become a rich resource of prosocial adults with whom young people can connect in meaningful ways. We become a village of adults who know and care about our young people. By developing meaningful connections with our students, we *will* become important adults in our students' lives without going beyond the expectations of our job descriptions as teachers.

3

Communicating to Our Students That We Care

It is Dale's first interview with me. The principal introduced us no more than fifteen minutes earlier. We begin to learn about each other by exchanging small talk, slowly working through the awkward feelings we all have when we first meet. Dale teases me about my "heavy equipment." I have two tape recorders going this time, one as a backup for the other. I no longer depend on my skills at speed typing as a fallback in case the tape recorder doesn't work. We start to chat about where Dale had trained to be a teacher and why he wanted to be a teacher. Sitting in a student's desk directly across from me, Dale appears relaxed, as if he is enjoying this opportunity to reflect on his background.

"What experiences have influenced your teaching?" I ask. Dale pauses for a few seconds, pondering that question, and then says, "Well, it's strange because when I was in high school, I had a math teacher who was as intimidating as hell. He just would use big words; he'd talk right at you. He'd make you break into a cold sweat just looking at him because he would intimidate you. And I thought then, 'I don't really think I'm learning a lot, feeling this way.' He was an outstanding man. I mean, he was smart, brilliant. But boy, he just really scared the living daylights out of me."

Dale pauses, and looks directly at me. "I want to make people feel at ease . . . and feel that they can do it—you know, that I'm not intimidating them in the field of math, like I felt when I talked to this man."

I remain silent while Dale recollects his thoughts and continues with his story. "We had another math teacher in my high school who was the father of three boys. Everybody called him 'Pops B___' because he was like a dad and he made you feel good. But boy, he earned your respect when you were in his class. He helped you feel like you could talk to him. You felt safe asking him anything, instead of feeling embarrassed to ask 'Why?' when you didn't understand. That is the only thing that I've really tried to carry with me—treat the kids with respect."

TREATING STUDENTS WITH DIGNITY AND RESPECT

No matter how hard we try to connect with students, if students do not interpret what we do as caring, close and trusting relationships will not develop. In order to develop caring relationships with our students, we need to be able to convey caring. In the example above, the intimidating, critical mathematics teacher Dale described may have cared deeply about students, but his mannerisms and nonverbal language kept his students at a distance. It is unlikely that he developed close and trusting relationships with students because students would have a hard time perceiving him as caring. Caring really is about a *way of being* in a relationship (Noddings, 1992). Although it does not emerge from a step-by-step formula, it does require a certain *way of being* in order for students to perceive our caring. The teachers I observed were able to *be* in relationships in such a way that students knew they cared. What is the way of being in relationships that helped students perceive these teachers as caring? Why did students believe that these teachers really cared?

Education literature has little to say about what teachers specifically do that communicates caring to their students. Parenting literature, though, is rich with research that provides insights into and guidance on communicating caring to children. Because a parent-child relationship is another example of an influential relationship (see Chapter 1), it seems reasonable to assume that the methods that facilitate perceptions of caring between parent and child would also facilitate perceptions of caring between teacher and student.

Drawing on research with parenting models, the behaviors and attitudes advocated by the authoritative parenting model have been empirically shown to increase feelings of closeness, caring, and trust between child and parent (McNabb, 1990). I believe this model can provide us with valuable insights into the ways of being in relationships that communicate caring to our students. In addition to communicating caring, the authoritative parenting approach also fosters self-reliance, self-control, a willingness to explore, and a sense of well-being in children (Baumrind, 1971a; Glenn, 1996; Hoffman, 1970). These are all qualities we would love to foster in our students also.

The Authoritative Parenting Model

In the authoritative parenting model, parents establish their authority but do not require unquestioning obedience. On a continuum with permissive parental responses on one end and authoritarian parental responses on the other, authoritative parenting behavior and responses fall right in the middle. The authoritative parenting model includes the following behaviors and attitudes:

1. Parents control their children through attempts to explain their rules and decisions and by reasoning with them.

2. Parents are willing to listen to their child's point of view, even if they do not always accept it.

3. Parents set high standards for their children's behavior and encourage them to be individualistic and independent.

4. Parents make demands of their children that are limited to what is developmentally appropriate for the child.

5. Parents affirm what is right about the child; they separate the child's personal worth from his or her behavior.

6. Parents use discipline as an opportunity to teach the child so he or she can internalize the learning and become independent (Baumrind, 1971b; Briggs, 1977; Cole & Cole, 1989; Glenn, 1996; Hoffman, 1970).

These parenting behaviors communicate thoughtfulness and respect for a child and promote the prosocial development of children (Baumrind, 1971b; Glenn, 1996; Glenn & Nelsen, 1988; Hoffman, 1970).

The Key to Conveying Caring

A key principle in the authoritative parenting model that conveys to children a parent's caring is that children are treated firmly, with dignity and respect (Glenn, 1996; Glenn & Nelsen, 1988). Treating children with dignity means honoring their position and their abilities and seeing them as worthy of esteem. Treating children with respect means showing regard for their basic human right of expression and believing in their ability to manage their own lives successfully. Respect requires listening and sincerely considering what children are saying. With authoritative parenting, it is taken for granted that parents "have more knowledge and skill, control more resources, and have more physical power than their children, but [parents] believe that the *rights of parents and children are reciprocal*" (Cole & Cole, 1989, p. 383). Reciprocity is a key word. Children are viewed as capable and significant and are treated respectfully (Glenn, 1996). They have reciprocal rights.

WAYS TO SHOW RESPECT FOR STUDENTS

The authoritative parenting model has helped parents develop close and trusting relationships with their children, and it can help us, too, in our efforts to communicate to our students that we care. When we believe our students have reciprocal rights, we use our power respectfully and ethically. Respectful treatment of students is the way of being in relationships with students that communicates caring.

The respectful way students were treated by the six teachers I observed was awe inspiring to watch. Whenever they spoke to and about students, these teachers used a considerate tone of voice and receptive manner. For instance, Tom addressed the students as *sirs* and *ladies*. Dale addressed them as *ladies* and *gentlemen:* "Ladies and gentlemen, I am glad to see you. I am really glad to see you. We need paper, pencils, and books today." These teachers also spoke respectfully *about* their students—even when their students were not around. They refused to join in the faculty lounge student "bashing" that often takes place.

Treating Students as Adults

All six teachers valued respect and worked for the respect of their students. For instance, at the beginning of the year Dale told his students, "I'm going to earn your respect. I'm going to work really hard to earn your respect. And I will respect you just as much as you respect me." All six teachers took time to listen to their students and take their concerns seriously. Pam disclosed to me her respectful feelings towards her students during an interview: "I relate to them as people . . . I don't talk down to kids. I never have, I don't think, in a condescending way." One day at lunch Dean disclosed to me, in a somewhat startling observation, the respect he felt towards his students at Inner City High. "These kids are adults," he said. "They've already made more decisions in their life than you or I have had to. You can't treat them like kids, but like adults." Dean then paused for a second, looked around the room and added, "Take for instance the kid sitting up there studying." He pointed to a small boy studying during his lunch period. "He's a gang member and has been faced with situations you or I haven't dreamed of."

Appreciating the difficult life situations their students cope with daily helped these teachers focus primarily on their students' strengths. They treated their students as adults—as people—not as objects that were frustrating because they did not do what they were supposed to do. Gail said, "I see them as little people. I see them as independent thinkers, as very nice people." She paused for a moment and then continued, "Even the ones who are sort of rough. They are really nice but you have to cut through the roughness to get to the nice part."

I asked the student teacher working with Tom to identify what Tom did to show students that he cared. Bill's reply was quick in coming. "I think it comes down to respect. There is a definite two-way respect in that classroom. You know, a lot of teachers expect the kids to respect them, but it's not reciprocated." As discussed in Chapter 2, Tom showed all students respect while keeping his expectations of his students high, even the special education students mainstreamed into his classroom.

It was clear the six teachers *assumed* that students were doing the best they could, given their developmental level and life circumstances, and in that light, all students deserved respect. And as a result of their respectful treatment of their students, these teachers gained their students' respect and appreciation.

Disciplining With Respect

We often view discipline as a necessary evil that comes along with our jobs as teachers. The caring teachers I observed saw discipline as a teachable moment—as an opportunity to be respectful of students, provide moral guidance, and promote student growth, rather than as a burden. They extended to students the opportunity to make their own mistakes and live with the consequences—without judgment. (See Resource 1: Discipline as Moral Guidance.) Approached in this way, discipline promotes a safe learning environment and creates powerful opportunities for teachers to treat students respectfully. During my observations, these teachers were never seen to use discipline for punishment or as a weapon in a power struggle with the students. Nor did the teachers discuss discipline in this manner. These teachers understood that classroom management and caring are threads from the same tapestry.

Tom provides a beautiful example of viewing discipline as a teachable moment. He had observed an "A" student cheating on an exam. Not singling her out, the next day he led a class discussion on cheating. He described cheating as compromising personal values of honesty and integrity. He discussed the choices students have and explained that they need not compromise their personal values when making choices. He talked about how students should make amends when they make inappropriate choices in order to stay congruent with their value systems. Then, at lunch, he quietly pulled the student aside and asked her a series of questions about her perception of her efforts with the examination. At first she did not admit to cheating. Tom told her what behavior he had observed when she was taking the test, without accusing her of cheating. She then quietly acknowledged cheating. Once cheating was established, Tom asked her to give some serious thought to her value system, to her views of right and wrong, and to how difficult it is to live up to that value system and how she wanted to make amends. He gave her another day to think about this, saying that he was not sure yet what he was going to do.

The next day the student was remorseful and honest. She acknowledged that she should be treated like anyone else who had been caught cheating. She got a zero on the test, dropping her tentative grade from an "A" to a "C." Tom said,

> You know you deserve respect for acknowledging that you should be treated like anyone else. I need to tell you that I'm going to call your parents, and that you'll have to spend two hours with me next Thursday after school as part of the punishment, just like anyone else would. I don't hate you. I don't dislike you. I don't think any less of you. You made a mistake. Just learn from this and make this a valuable experience and everything will work out.

Using Humor When We Discipline

Handling discipline with humor is a congenial way to treat students respectfully while identifying inappropriate behavior. I have many examples from my classroom observations of these teachers using gentle humor.

> Gail quiets the class down to begin work. "The more time you spend getting things together now, the more homework you will have to do tonight." She then says teasingly, "Any group who does the best work will get Rudolph's sandwich." "Oh no!" Rudolph cries. "You can't do that . . . I'll sue." Everyone laughs and Rudolph beams. The class then quiets down and begins working.

> Tom goes over to a student who is making fun of him and places his hands on the student's shoulders to quiet him down. The student asks him to mess up his hair. Tom ruffles the student's hair and then looks disgustedly at his hand. "What weight of oil is that, 10 weight?" Everyone laughs.

> Dale calls on a student who was not paying attention. "Matthew, what answer did you get for this problem?" Matthew says, "I don't understand how to divide this." Dale gently says, "Watch me and maybe you will get it." Matthew says, "I don't want to copy." Dale laughs. "I'm the guy in class that you can copy." Dale turns to me and says, "Matthew has a reputation for copying. We used to call him Xerox."

> Dale asks the students to work on a problem. Everyone starts working quietly. Students begin asking one another for help.

The noise picks up. Dale says, "Don't shout out the answer because you will spoil all the fun for Erica, Jane, and Mary." The girls laugh. The class quiets down again.

The deep level of respect these teachers showed exemplifies honoring students wherever they are in their development. None of the caring teachers were *nicey-nice* to students. Being permissive, sweet, warm, or gentle is *not* a prerequisite of caring. In fact, two of the caring teachers were stern and strict, and two appeared detached and aloof, but they were respectful. Students saw all of them as caring. These teachers provide us with compelling examples—not only of respectful treatment of students but of ways to use the inherent power of our positions ethically. (See Resource 2: Treating Students With Dignity and Respect.)

Handling Our Own Discipline Problems

Curiously, the observed teachers seldom used the formal discipline system within their schools. Some of them *never* used the school discipline system. "I may have sent two or three people in about thirteen years [to the office]. I try to handle it myself," said Gail. Dean also saw discipline as solely his responsibility. "I don't even think of the discipline policies. You know why? Because what happens with me is within *my* classroom. I do my own discipline." Dean felt if he could not deal with the situation effectively, the administration would not be able to either. Ruby said, "[Discipline] is between the teacher and the student. It's not like for every little [discipline problem] you have to run outside the classroom and pull in an administrator. There's a lot that is left up to your discretion to deal with that student one-to-one, which I think is good." Pam explained why she chose to use the formal discipline system as the last resort. "I use [infractions] as the last resort . . . the kids don't take them seriously. Part of the reason kids don't take them seriously is that some teachers use them too readily. They rely on the system as the first consequence." Tom volunteered to be in charge of afterschool detention. He said, "It gives me a way to connect with some of the tough students," and he was able to work with his own students. Dale made the students walk around the building if they acted up. He seldom used formal discipline channels because he did not agree with the discipline policies and procedures. His students said they were applied unfairly. Dale said, "I don't think I agree with suspensions. Then it just gets the kid out of school."

Assuming responsibility for disciplining students rather than depending on the school's formal discipline system is another way these teachers communicated respect to their students. By managing their own discipline problems, these teachers were communicating that they believed in the student's ability and willingness to self-correct. If the teacher and student worked together, they could resolve the problem.

Disciplining our own students provides an additional benefit; it clearly defines our role of authority in the teacher-student relationship. Without a doubt, the teacher is identified as the change agent in the influential relationship with the students. Thus discipline helps us to maintain appropriate professional boundaries with our students by emphasizing our authority and clarifying our role with students.

Creating a Culturally Relevant Environment

Particularly for students of color, a respectful environment is also a culturally relevant environment. Teachers with classrooms composed primarily of students of color can create a culturally relevant classroom environment by providing curriculum that reflects the cultures of the students (Ladson-Billings, 1992). Culturally relevant teaching requires the recognition of minority cultures as valuable experiences upon which to build classroom curriculum. In doing so, students are respected and celebrated both as individuals and as members of a specific culture. Students can experiment with new behaviors for social change with encouragement and support while critically examining society.

Gail, at Inner City High School, provided an example of a culturally relevant curriculum. Her readings in literature often had people of color as primary characters or in lead roles. She drew her examples from minority cultures. For instance, the first day I observed Gail her students were reading a selection from the book *Farewell to Manzanar*, which is about a Japanese American family. The second day of observation, students were analyzing Martin Luther King, Jr.'s "I Have a Dream" speech. The third day I observed Gail, students were reading a play about African Americans written in the dialect of the late nineteenth century. (See Resource 3: Creating a Safe Learning Environment.)

HOW STUDENTS RESPOND TO RESPECTFUL TREATMENT

Students' positive responses to respectful treatment document the power of treating students with dignity and respect. Students who were treated respectfully responded respectfully. They recognized they were being treated as assets rather than objects. Rosie, a student of Dean's, discussed how being treated respectfully promotes respect. She said, "Well, everyone respects [Dean]. Like, if people don't respect the teacher, and the teacher tells us to do [something] we'll just talk back and then the teacher will have to make us leave or something . . . and we won't care." Students did not talk back to Dean. They quietly did whatever he asked of them. A student of Tom's defined this dynamic succinctly when asked why students did not resist whatever Tom asked them to do: "We treat him with respect because he treats us with respect."

Tom's student teacher, Bill, shared a compelling vignette depicting Tom teaching through discipline and how student attitudes and behavior were affected by such respectful treatment. Tom had a substitute teacher take over his class one day when he had to attend a conference. Bill described the mayhem that happened and how Tom handled the situation the following day. (We are all familiar with how rough junior high school students can be on a substitute teacher!)

> The kids *ate [the substitute] alive . . .* they just *ate this guy alive!* It was pathetic. The kids were on a feeding frenzy! Early the next morning, I mentioned it to Tom. He was furious! Tom doesn't like his class acting like that. He confronted the class with the information I had shared, but he did it in a real interesting way. He didn't tell them I told him. He said, "I hear there were some problems yesterday. What were they?" The kids immediately started confessing. And it wasn't Jimmy telling on Susie or Susie telling on Bobby. The kids who had been the problem students said, "I did this." It was the damnedest thing! Their honest response showed me that they have a whole heck of a lot of respect for Tom because when they were caught, they didn't try to weasel out of it. And they didn't give excuses, like, "Well, I did it because . . ." They just said, "I did it." No prompting, no threatening. I don't know how he got them to that point. It was amazing. I had given him the names of the perpetrators, but they all owned up!

Tom calmly and clearly expressed his disappointment with his students. He had Bill, his student teacher, share how embarrassed he felt observing the class behave so discourteously to the substitute teacher. Then, together, Tom and his students worked out a plan to ensure that it would not happen again. He treated the students like adults and taught them problem-solving skills. Tom's respectful disappointment was enough punishment to modify the behavior of his students.

How Respect Affects Student Learning

Students of the caring teachers appeared to thrive as learners in the caring environment provided for them. They were open to paying attention and motivated to try. When students are treated respectfully, they care about how they are doing in class. Annette, a student of Dale's, provides a powerful documentation of how respect affects learning. A troubled student with an alcohol problem, Annette communicated that she felt respected by Dale, in spite of her shortcomings. She related this respect in the following way:

> After being suspended for a while you come back and it's like totally weird being in school again. And, you know, I walked

in [Dale's] classroom and he's like, 'Hey Annette! You're back! Congratulations, you made it!' You know, he is like, 'Have a seat. Come on. We're waiting for you' and stuff. You know, he like *welcomed* me.

A minute later in the interview, she admitted to trying harder and doing better in Dale's classes.

I mean, he's the only math teacher I've learned from. I'm good at math but I usually don't get good grades in it. All my life I've gotten D's and stuff, and this year I'm finally getting B's in his class.

Annette clearly saw that Dale cared about her, and her perception of his caring clearly influenced her learning and academic growth.

As teachers, it is reassuring to know that students who feel respected by us will reciprocate with respect and will try harder with their studies. And it is rewarding to know that student motivation and achievement are increased simply by our genuine caring. (See Resource 4: Student Recognition of and Reaction to Respectful Treatment.)

Student Receptiveness to a Teacher's Caring

Treating students with dignity and respect may be the key to promoting not only a student's ability to perceive our caring but also his or her *receptiveness* to that caring. As evidenced by responses on student inventories, the students of the six teachers described in this study were open and receptive to their caring. Students shared their thoughts and ideas, even about sensitive situations, with these teachers. They knew their teacher would listen to their concerns, hear their side of a story, and respond fairly when dealing with them. They trusted their teacher would help them with school problems. They felt safe turning to the teacher when they needed help. Treated respectfully, they felt safe being open and receptive to their teacher's caring. (See Resource 5: Student Receptiveness to and Perception of a Teacher's Caring.) To find out how open and receptive your students are to your caring, try giving your students the Student Inventory (Figure 3.1).

SUMMARY OF HOW WE COMMUNICATE CARING

Treating students with dignity and respect is *key* for communicating caring to students. It is the principle that cuts across all my data. When being respectful, we communicate caring to students at all times—when disciplining them, correcting their assignments, lecturing, or playing

Figure 3.1   Student Inventory

STUDENT INVENTORY

Please describe your relationship with your teacher. Fill in each blank with the number that comes closest to how you think or feel. Please put NA if the statement does not apply to you.

1	2	3	4	5	6
Strongly Agree					Strongly Disagree

_____ I feel close to and trust this teacher.

_____ I feel my teacher listens to my concerns when I talk to him or her.

_____ My teacher has qualities that I would like to develop within myself.

_____ Even when I schedule time to talk to my teacher, I get the feeling I am taking too much of his or her time.

_____ My teacher has high expectations of me, but I am capable of achieving them.

_____ When I have done something wrong, my teacher doesn't listen to my side.

_____ I trust that my teacher will help when I need help with school problems.

_____ I do not like my teacher.

_____ My teacher embarrasses me for not knowing the right answer.

_____ My teacher is fair in dealing with students with their school problems.

_____ In solving classroom problems, students' suggestions are honored.

_____ I do not look forward to being in this teacher's classroom.

_____ If some of my friends wanted me to ignore a classmate and my teacher asked me to help this classmate with homework, I would do what my friends wanted me to do.

_____ I do not feel safe sharing my thoughts and feelings with my teacher.

_____ My teacher can control the classroom without embarrassing any students.

_____ My teacher is interested in what I do outside of his or her classroom.

_____ I do not feel respected by this teacher.

_____ This teacher does not help me to enjoy learning.

_____ I usually enjoy school.

_____ I feel my teacher really cares about me as a person.

_____ I enjoy/would enjoy spending free time with my teacher.

with them. Treating students with dignity and respect enhances students' perception, receptivity, and trust in the teacher's caring and concern, and creates a safe learning environment that supports and motivates student achievement.

How to Score the Student Inventory Worksheet

You score this inventory by tallying the scores for each statement and then reviewing the results to identify your strong points and the areas in which you might improve. A low total score (1 or 2 times the number of participants) indicates your area of strength. A high score (5 or 6 times the number of participants) indicates areas for professional growth.

4

What It Takes to Revitalize Ourselves

Dean is sitting in a chair cattycorner from me, using the large library table next to us as an armrest. It is lunchtime. The Inner City High School library is mostly unoccupied, except for students who intermittently enter and stop to chat with Dean. Between interruptions Dean is intensely focused on the interview, animatedly answering the questions. He seems to radiate an energy that is contagious. This is my first interview with Dean. I have not yet observed him teach.

"Any thoughts of leaving the teaching profession?" I ask.

"I thought about counseling," Dean responds. "I really truly believe that there is going to be a time in my life when I'm not going to be as effective with kids . . . when it's time to let the younger person do the actual teaching part, and me do more of a support role. At sixty years old, leading a classroom can take the life out of you. When you come observe these kids, you'll realize you've got to give a lot of energy if you're going to make it happen. At sixty years old, I'm not going to be able to do that. I know I'm going to want to be in a support role. I know that." Silently I nod in acknowledgment, although inwardly I wonder if a counselor's role is any easier.

Dean leans forward and continues to talk, animatedly waving his hands. "Since I've been here, I swear to God, there's only one person in my entire six years that has retired on a nonmedical. All eight of the other people were medical. They had heart problems. Oh my God! They just reached this frazzled point. They hauled this one dude out on a stretcher. I'm not lying! On a stretcher! I remember because he grabbed the principal and said, 'It was that f___ English class!' He had been a math teacher. For years he taught math and driver's ed and they made him teach an English class! They needed someone to teach English 101." Dean chuckles, "It was almost funny after he got better. He came back and retired at the end of the year. The dude just said, 'I can't do this anymore. I'm leaving on a medical leave before I kill myself.'"

HOW WE CAN REVITALIZE OURSELVES

Clearly, if we are to provide care and attention to students we need ways to support and revitalize ourselves. Research literature shows that relationships involving mutual give-and-take are sources of rich emotional rewards for individuals, but we know that the teacher-student relationship is not one in which there is a mutual give-and-take (Heifetz & Bersani, 1983). Teachers give more. As caregivers in influential relationships, we are expected to give even when we receive little in return. We are presumed to be more mature and more capable of dealing with the world. The asymmetrical nature of our relationships with students is an emotional drain. It is not the heavy emotional involvement with students that drains us, but rather the intense involvement with little dividends (Heifetz & Bersani, 1983). Consistently caring without consistent returns creates an imbalance in the caring cycle—the mutual giving and receiving of caring—and is the root of emotional burnout.

Understandably, we can be worn down by this lack of completion in the caring cycle when working closely with 150 students. So how did the six teachers I observed sustain and revitalize their personal and professional energies? How did these teachers maintain their enthusiasm for their jobs year after year? To shed some light on these concerns, I quizzed my teachers about the ways they replenished their professional energy, listening closely to what they said. I also explored the literature on burnout prevention for teachers. What I read gave me new insights into self-care and prevention of burnout. With the literature providing a theoretical framework, I identified the personal traits and skills these teachers held in common that enabled them to work at such an intense level *and* still get emotional rewards. Some of us may already be familiar with resources and strategies for revitalization, and this chapter will only reassure and reinforce what we already know. Others, like me, may gain additional insights for self-care. But, most important, those of us contemplating taking a more active nurturing role in the lives of our students, or who have already assumed such a role, will feel more confident about our decision if we know ways to keep ourselves revitalized and inspired.

REWARDS AND FEELING COMPETENT

Research shows that feeling competent and effective in our chosen careers helps alleviate stress (Farber, 1991). Feeling competent about our teaching abilities and confident that we can achieve our goals for teaching can be a rich source of renewal for us. Thus if we value making a difference for students, the cornerstone of our efforts to sustain our professional energy is first, knowing that a caring relationship with a prosocial adult is the key and second, feeling competent in our ability to make such caring connections. Any personal resource that enhances our ability to achieve our goals as teachers can be a source of renewal for us.

The teachers I observed *wanted* caring connections with their students and they *were* competent at making those connections. At the same time, these teachers maintained a lot of enthusiasm and energy, even after years of being on the job. When interviewing the six teachers in my study, the personal revitalizing resources they held in common became apparent:

Expansive beliefs about teaching

Personal qualities that enhance connecting with students

Relational skills that enhance connecting with students

Knowing about these personal revitalizing resources gives us insight into what helped these teachers feel competent at making connections— and thus sustained their enthusiasm for their jobs. In turn, for those of us interested in maintaining our professional energies as caring teachers, awareness of these resources gives us some qualities and skills to strive for within ourselves. Most of the personal revitalizing resources identified are ethereal in nature and therefore difficult to illustrate through brief examples, but the pervasiveness of each of the personal resources is documented by brief examples or quotes from each teacher. These can be found in the Resources section at the end of the book.

BELIEFS ABOUT THE ROLE OF TEACHERS AND TEACHING

Observations and interviews with the six caring teachers revealed six commonly held beliefs about teachers and the teaching profession:

1. Student growth and maturation is the key educational goal.
2. The purpose of teaching is to be of service and make a difference for young people.
3. Teachers must handle their power ethically.
4. Curriculum is a means of promoting student growth.
5. Teaching is a valued and valuable profession.
6. Classroom teaching is more fulfilling than administrative work.

These six beliefs or values about the teaching profession were strongly shared by all the teachers and inspired and motivated their desire to develop caring connections with students. Holding these beliefs, and being able to successfully act according to them, gives these teachers the emotional rewards they need for the work they do. These beliefs give direction and purpose to a caring teacher's desire to take a more active and supportive role in the lives of their students and make a difference for young people.

Belief One: Student Growth and Maturation Is the Key Educational Goal

All six teachers in my study identified their number-one goal for education as some variation of promoting student growth and maturity. Like McLaughlin and Talbert (1990), who polled nurturing teachers and discovered that their most valued educational goal was the personal growth of students, I polled the teachers I observed using the same choices for educational goals. I discovered the same results. I asked the teachers in my study to rank the following educational goals:

Basic academic skills

Good work habits

Academic excellence

Personal growth

Human relations skills

Citizenship

Occupational skills

Moral and ethical maturation

Four of the teachers chose personal growth as the most important educational goal, one teacher ranked it as second after moral and ethical development, and one teacher ranked it third, after moral and ethical development and citizenship. Even the choices of the latter two teachers demonstrate their concern about the personal growth and maturation of students above academic excellence and basic academic skills. Because they believe the personal, emotional, and moral development of students is the key educational goal, the observed teachers could more easily commit their professional time, energy, and curricula to nurturing students. For teachers who hold such a holistic view of teaching, nurturing students is a natural outcome.

Although these teachers viewed their role as including responsibility for the social, emotional, and moral growth of students, they did not hold this view at the expense of their primary responsibilities as teachers—the academic outcomes and cognitive development of students. A commitment to social, emotional, and moral development of students does not preclude a commitment to student academic growth. They did not see cognitive development occurring independently of social, emotional, and moral development. Rather they believed social, moral, emotional, and cognitive development happened synergistically. In other words, they viewed the academic growth of students as part and parcel of their goal for student personal growth and maturation. As Dean said,

> I think that the bottom line for all teachers who are nurturing is that you really care about your student outcomes, what happens to every one of your students—when you start and when you finish with them. Everything else is like a different means to the same ends . . . a better individual.

Dale provides evidence of these teachers' overall commitment to their students' academic achievement by his willingness to teach a basic mathematics course, Fundamentals of Mathematics. Dale saw too many basic mathematics students failing the competency test, and he believed these students could learn mathematics. He wanted to try some new teaching strategies to help them learn the subject. The year I observed him was his first year of teaching Fundamentals of Mathematics in his fourteen years of teaching. "I don't have a textbook because I feel that that's the same old thing they've always done," he said. "So I'm trying to do new things, to be real creative with those guys. I create things as I go in that class. What I do is, like on Sunday evenings, I'll come in and plan my week."

Dean gives another good example of his commitment to student academic achievement in his willingness to spend personal money to provide his students with the important learning materials they need to understand the topic. "Man, I probably spend fifteen hundred dollars a year out of my own pocket just to buy everything! We have no budget." He laughs. "Today we looked at jellyfish. I had to buy those jellyfish. The next thing we look at is squid, and I'm going to have to go down and buy squid. For a lot of things, like jellyfish, I have to send to a biological supply house, and that's like a bank!" (See Resource 6: Commitment to Student Learning for additional examples.)

Belief Two: The Purpose of Teaching Is to Be of Service and Make a Difference

With a primary educational goal of promoting student growth and maturation, these teachers broadly view educators as human service professionals. All six teachers were motivated to become teachers to be of service to others in a meaningful way and make a difference for young people. This value was strongly held by all six teachers. Tom says,

> Probably the thing that attracted me most to teaching was the desire to try and have some kind of influence on bettering our society . . . teaching gives me the opportunity to have what I think is a tremendous impact upon the future.

Monetary rewards were not a major consideration for any of the teachers. In fact, Pam and Dean changed careers as adults, leaving well-paid positions in the business world to return to college and become teachers. Both were seeking careers that satisfied a personal need to be of service to others and make a difference. When Dale was asked what his purpose was as a teacher, he said, "to turn that light on in each kid. We used to call it 'your paycheck.' You get a paycheck when that kid's eyes light up, 'I got it. I understand!' That's the paycheck." Tom summarized the motivation by saying, "Money isn't the overall motivation in life. There's satisfaction in helping someone. You're not paid for everything." (See Resource 7: Personal Motivation to Be a Teacher for brief examples.)

Belief Three: Teachers Must Handle Their Power Ethically

The observed teachers were keenly aware of the powerful effect they had on students' lives. They acknowledged the power their actions, words, and attitudes have on young, developing human beings. They believed it was the moral and ethical responsibility of teachers to be aware of how they used that power. They recognized that how they interacted with students influenced a student's self-perception and self-esteem and was key in making a difference for students.

Gail related a story of how she became aware of her power as a teacher when using the blue eyes/brown eyes experiment. In this experiment, a teacher arbitrarily pigeonholes all students with a specific eye color as inferior, ignorant, second-class citizens. Students with the other eye color are considered superior, bright, and capable. The teacher interacts and reacts to students according to the labels. It is a powerful experiential exercise used to demonstrate stereotyping. After using this exercise, Gail was keenly aware of the responsibility she carried with her power as a teacher.

> We have a lot of power, a lot of power. Teachers don't realize it until they've done something damaging or until someone has come back after ten years and said, 'I've become this because of you.' I didn't recognize it really, until four years ago when I did an experiment with my class—the blue-eyed/brown-eyed experiment. It took me about seven minutes to make half the kids really mad, really upset, and doubt their abilities. *About seven minutes!* And these are kids that I've had for four or five months and just that fast I was able to make them think they were stupid, and they couldn't do well on

tests and the other side of the room was better than they were. It took me another twenty minutes to tell them that this was all a test, not for real.

As a child, Ruby was powerfully impacted by the teachers in her life. So was Tom. They knew the power of a teacher from firsthand experience, and they knew that a single teacher can make a difference in students' lives. They recognized they had the same powerful role in shaping the future of their students. (See Resource 8: Power of the Position for brief examples.)

Belief Four: Curriculum Is a Means of Promoting Student Growth

These caring teachers did not believe that the content knowledge they held so dearly was the most important lesson they taught their students. Teaching students how to lead productive lives and become better people was more important. They viewed their subject matter as a vehicle to influence student growth and maturity. It was simply a means to an end. The end purpose for these teachers was to help students function successfully in society as prosocial human beings. Dean said,

A kid's got to be able to read; a kid's got to be able to write; a kid's got to be able to do math; but he's also got to be able to work in a group; he's got to be able to respect his peers and deal with people, even people he doesn't like or she doesn't like.

Waving his hand in the air as if to make the point stronger, Dean continued, "They've got to be able to have pride in themselves and self-respect, and a real pride and respect in their community and the people around them." He paused and then added,

My whole approach to teaching is to take a person and use the academic part to direct all of this—the reading and writing and the math and stuff like that. I use biology as the vehicle to try to make those other things occur—self-respect, all that kind of stuff.

Pam reflected the same sentiments as Dean. While strict about the academic quality of her students' work, she said, "I mean, I love history and I believe it's real wonderful and all that. But is a seventh grader's life really going to change if they know who the rulers of Mesopotamia are? No." She paused to collect her thoughts.

What's more important is that they learn how to be successful as people and they learn how to get along with each other. You know, they learn how to retrieve information that they are going to need. They learn how to work cooperatively. Those are some of the things important to me in teaching kids . . . that they have a sense of responsibility about being citizens and contributing and about being human beings and having compassion for one another. That's a lot more important to me.

(See Resource 9: Subject as a Vehicle for brief examples.)

Belief Five: Teaching Is a Valued and Valuable Profession

These teachers valued their profession and perceived the teaching profession as valued by others. They were advocates for the profession. They demonstrated their commitment to the profession by their pride in their level of expertise and their continual efforts to upgrade their skills and knowledge in order to become better teachers.

All the observed teachers had a high level of expertise in their content area and worked to stay abreast of new developments in their chosen subjects. For example, Pam said,

> I have a very confident grasp of the subject. I bring to this more depth and a broader knowledge base than—this is going to sound conceited, but—almost everybody, well, certainly in this building. And that's just because I've read history for almost all of my life, certainly all of my adult life. And I think about it in different ways and how it can be applied.

Ruby also was proud of her expertise in the subject area in which she teaches. Proudly she said, "I am knowledgeable about what it is that I teach."

All these teachers were lifelong learners, actively seeking new learning experiences for professional growth. Dale and Gail regularly attended conferences and workshops available to them, or took university courses to build their skills as teachers. Dean had traveled out of state to a large prestigious university for summer studies in biology. He had recently been selected as an exchange teacher to Japan. He saw this experience as giving him a different perspective and new insights for teaching science. Tom was a social activist. He was energized by school renewal efforts and stayed on the cutting edge of school reform within his building and his district. He was working on implementing team teaching and was designing curriculum to teach to multiple types of intelligence. Such enthusiasm for their subjects and their profession made these teachers good stewards of the profession. They saw themselves as professionals and they continued to grow professionally. (See Resource 10: Viewing Themselves as Professionals for brief examples.)

Belief Six: Classroom Teaching Is
More Fulfilling Than Administrative Work

None of these teachers had an interest in becoming an administrator. They planned to remain in the classroom or in direct service to students their whole careers. Not only were they not interested in advancing in their careers through the administrative channels, but they all stated quite passionately their distaste for administrative positions. Here are some examples of responses when asked if they ever thought of being an administrator:

Tom: You could never get me to be an administrator. I don't have the personality for that. I don't have the patience. I have patience for kids but man, you put me in a room with parents not willing to do a thing and they're chewing on you because you suspended their kid for doing something—NO WAY! I won't do that. I'd rather shoot myself before I become an administrator.

Gail: No! No! No! I have no desire to be an administrator. It involves too much politics and not enough kids.

Ruby: I wouldn't touch that with a ten-foot pole. I think administration, especially when you come in at entry level and start out as a vice-principal, that so much of the contact with kids is the discipline. I don't think I would get a lot of positives from working with kids like that. In the classroom you are going to deal with things like that but on a much, much smaller basis. The positive contact you have with the kids will greatly outweigh that. I am going to stay put in the classroom.

All the teachers I observed responded to this question similarly. These teachers enjoyed working closely with kids in a classroom. Foremost, they valued the relationship with young people and did not see administrative positions as offering them the same opportunities for connecting with kids that teaching offers. For these teachers, the relationship with young people was truly what gave their profession meaning. They had no desire to move up an educational career ladder to an administrative position.

Summary of Personal Beliefs as Inner Resources

Common personal beliefs about teaching and the role of a teacher provided the observed teachers with a fundamental direction and gave a clear purpose to their caring behavior. The beliefs provided them with a coherent value system that gave them cognitive support for their desire to make healthy connections with students. In return, feeling competent at making such connections gave them the emotional rewards they needed to replenish their professional energy. These teachers became teachers in order to make a difference for students. The pervasive awareness and acknowledgment that they *can and do* make a difference helped to nurture these teachers and completed the caring cycle for them. For those of us who also want to make a difference for our students, focusing on the beliefs we hold that give direction and purpose to our efforts to make a difference will help sustain our professional energies as well.

PERSONAL QUALITIES THAT ENHANCE CONNECTING WITH STUDENTS

Besides holding in common beliefs about the role of a teacher and the teaching profession, these teachers also held in common several personal qualities that enhanced their ability to make and maintain positive, meaningful connections with their students. By increasing their ability to reach their teaching goals, these personal qualities helped them maintain their enthusiasm and professional energy:

1. Genuineness
2. Tolerance for imperfection
3. Sense of personal accountability
4. Tolerance for ambiguity
5. Nonjudgmental attitude
6. Sense of humor
7. Ability to personally detach

Having these personal characteristics made it easier not only to develop healthy connections with their students, but also to keep in balance the demands required of such relationships. As we read about these personal qualities, we may identify some of our own strengths. Other qualities identified may give us ideas for areas in which we want to improve as we strive to develop our personal resources for revitalization.

Quality One: Genuineness

The personal quality that stood out most vividly early in the analysis was the genuineness of the teachers. Genuineness is defined as being fully and freely ourselves without overwhelming other individuals (Carkhuff, 1987). None of the six nurturing teachers presented a façade or phoniness that would misrepresent them. They did not hide behind their position as teacher to define themselves in relation to their students. They presented themselves to students first as human beings and second as teachers. They appeared disarmingly unpretentious and unaffected. This personal quality facilitates making connections because it engenders trust and increases approachability. Genuineness on the teacher's part promotes like responses in students and cultivates trust and self-acceptance in individuals (Carkhuff, 1969, 1987; Rogers, 1961). As we improve our ability to be genuine and authentic, we enhance our competence in making meaningful connections with students. Here are some examples of genuineness as revealed by the teachers:

> Ruby pauses during a lecture and says, "Gosh, I am talking a lot. Am I talking too much?" she asks the class. Some in the class respond "no" and others respond "yes." Ruby listens to the feedback and says, "I hear several yeses, so let's move on." She moves to a group activity.

> Tom asks, "How many of you would find it hard not to strike back at someone who is hitting you?" Students raise their hands. Tom acknowledges that he would have a hard time also.

> A student asked Dale why he always writes two math problems on the board for the class to work out rather than just one. Dale humorously rattled off a series of reasons, "I am on a roll; besides, I don't want to break up my thought process and this is easier." Then he paused for a second, and said sincerely, "Actually, I don't have a real valid reason." He laughed and so did the students.

These teachers made a conscious choice to be genuine. Dean said, "No matter what you do you have to be honest. You have to be yourself. You have to show them yourself. Your teaching style has to be you. If I try to be anything but myself, I am not going to be a nurturing, caring type teacher. If I try to be something different it would just fail." Stressing the same point, Pam said, "To develop nurturing relationships with students you've got to be yourself. Don't try to force anything because kids can smell bullshit a mile away." Students acknowledged the genuineness of these teachers. When describing qualities he liked in Gail, a student said, "It's really hard to explain. You'd have to see it for yourself. You can't really put it into words. It's a lot—it's a lot in just watching her be herself." As we improve our ability to be genuine and authentic we will enhance our ability to make meaningful connections with students. (See also Resource 11: Genuineness for brief examples.)

Quality Two: Tolerance for Imperfection

These teachers did not expect themselves to be perfect or to react to students in the perfect way. They quickly acknowledged their mistakes, made verbal amends, and moved on to finding solutions. In fact, these teachers viewed mistakes as opportunities to learn and welcomed feedback that helped them to improve. Making and easily admitting mistakes helps "level the playing field" between teacher and student. We appear more approachable to students, thus it becomes easier to make positive teacher-student connections.

Many of us, though, have the need to be perfect. It is ironic that for caring teachers who want everything to be just right, *not* needing to be perfect is what increases our effectiveness in our jobs. In addition to increasing our competence, being at ease making and admitting mistakes alleviates the intense stress created by the need to be perfect. Developing an acceptance of imperfections within ourselves is an important step towards mediating stress.

Pam provided a vivid example of accepting her imperfections when she acknowledged to students that she was guilty of harassing a student the very day she led a discussion on harassment (see Chapter 2). Pam sent a student who had picked at a hangnail until it bled to the nurse's station to get a band aid. She began to joke around about how she hated blood. Several students joined in. They started poking fun at the triviality of the "injury," making fun of the student for wanting medical attention for a hangnail. Suddenly one student noted that they were harassing the student. "We are doing the very same thing we were talking about." Everyone was immediately quiet. There was a pregnant pause as students realized the truth in the statement. Then Pam said, "I was doing it too. What a jerk you have for a teacher!" A student piped up, "A cool jerk."

The observed teachers laughed at their mistakes, an attitude that helped them release stress. For instance, one observation day Dale made a mistake in the solution to a math problem he put on the board. After a few minutes the students started complaining that the problem was impossible. Dale glanced at the board and said, "Oh no! I forgot to carry over!" He went to the board and changed the numbers in the problem. The class groaned and playfully shouted, "You made a mistake. You are the math teacher! You are supposed to know this stuff." Dale laughed and said, "Yes, I made a mistake." The students laughed and teased, "When we make a mistake you count it against us. How come it doesn't count against you?" Dale teased back, "It does count against me. I have to put up with you guys raggin' on me. Isn't that enough?" The students all laughed. (See Resource 12: Accountability for Mistakes for brief examples.)

Quality Three: Sense of Personal Accountability

Teachers who maintain enthusiasm for their jobs have a sense of being personally accountable for what happens in their world. Having a sense of personal accountability means *assuming responsibility* for whatever happens in our lives. It is believing that our destinies are our own responsibilities and not controlled by other people or external events. And when fate hands us a difficult situation, it means we can recognize we are responsible for *our reactions* to the situation and proceed without blaming others for what is happening (Farber, 1991).

The caring teachers in the study did not accuse or blame the administration, students, or anyone else for the negative events that were happening in their professional lives. They acknowledged responsibility for the decisions they made that created change or turmoil, and they assumed responsibility for their reactions to events brought about by fate. In addition, they were not easily swayed from a personal conviction by the disapproval of others. They knew who they were, what they valued, and why their values were important to them.

A sense of personal accountability has been identified as the key characteristic of individuals who are least likely to experience stress and burnout (Farber, 1991; Fielding, 1982; Marlin, 1987; McIntyre, 1984). It is the key quality that we need to develop in order to mediate stress in our lives. Being personally accountable places the control of events or reactions to events squarely in our hands. With a sense of personal accountability, we recognize our *reaction* to stressful events is *our* responsibility and thus we can take charge and adopt strategies to alleviate our stress.

This sense of personal accountability supports us in our efforts to make close and trusting relationships with students simply by enabling us to enjoy our connections with students without always needing students to like us or respond positively to us. The observed teachers knew they were responsible for their caring responses and reactions to students, but they also knew they were not responsible for how their students responded to their caring efforts. What a freeing thought! The observed teachers understood that not all students would react positively to their efforts at caring. They simply enjoyed their connections with students without necessarily expecting a completion to the caring cycle.

Gail provides an example of a sense of personal accountability. She said, "If I have a class that is either not focused or not managed the way I like to see it managed, then I take responsibility for that. I need to find out what to do to manage it or what I need to do to help students get focused." She added, "I've been around teachers who always put the blame on the child, the child's home, and this and that. My daughter's teacher is that way, where it's, 'Well, she plays around and she does this or she does that.' My question to her is, 'What have you done to make her attentive? Have you changed your plans? Have you changed your classroom management style?'" (See Resource 13: Sense of Personal Accountability for brief examples.)

Quality Four: Tolerance for Ambiguity

Although a sense of control is an important factor for stress management, being able to deal comfortably with situations out of one's control is just as essential. When jobs demand working with a variety of people on a variety of projects, like teaching, a tolerance for ambiguity is essential (Fielding, 1982). The observed teachers understood that not everything was within their control, nor was it clearly defined, but they also understood their *reaction* to any situation was always in their control. When necessary, they could comfortably let go of control and adapt to ambiguous situations.

Developing a tolerance for ambiguity requires reframing what is important to us. It requires that we not always be in control, which is often difficult for teachers. We like being in control. Some of us may need to seek professional counseling to learn to be comfortable letting go of control. Although it may be hard work to develop tolerance for ambiguity, the rewards are well worth it. Going home energized and revitalized after a particularly haphazard day would certainly help sustain our careers as caring teachers.

Dean and Dale were masters at tolerating ambiguity. Their skills were demonstrated by how quickly they shifted gears and moved from one student's demand to the next. They had a high tolerance for confusion, noise, and disorganization. Not only were they tolerant of these environments, they thrived in them. I remember one day, after observing Dean all day, I had a headache. My ears were ringing. The students had been unusually loud and boisterous, excited about their biology projects, running around the classroom. I was packing up my computer, looking forward to a nice quiet evening at home, when Dean came charging into the classroom with a big grin on his face. "I love days like today," he said. "I just love days like today. Weren't the students just great and the assignment went so well? This is why I teach! I get so much energy from days like this." I looked at him in disbelief. He was excited and energized. After a particularly frazzling day, with many different unplanned events happening, Dean was energized!

Both Dean and Dale can remain focused in the midst of the confusion, responding to a variety of student questions seemingly at the same time. For instance, I observed Dale teaching a student assistant how to fix a computer glitch while asking one student to sit properly in her desk and suggesting another student use a calculator. Dale did all this without losing his focus on the problem he was explaining to the student assistant.

A tolerance for ambiguity helps to reduce stress by increasing our adaptability to a variety of situations. It seems particularly helpful for those teachers who choose to make connections with students primarily through one-to-one time during class time. Creating one-to-one time with students requires that teachers are able to shift gears quickly and thrive in environments where many different demands are being made. It requires that we enjoy doing a multitude of tasks at what seems to be the same time and have little quiet, focused concentration time—at least during the actual class period. A tolerance for ambiguity lets these demands become opportunities, not emotional drains.

Quality Five: Nonjudgmental Attitude

A nonjudgmental attitude means an individual does not shame or accentuate what is wrong with another person, but rather recognizes the person is doing the best that he or she can at a given moment. As noted before, being naturally nonjudgmental, these teachers saw a student's potential, not imperfections. They were able to focus on what was good about a student even when the student's behavior was inappropriate. They did not raise their voices or criticize students when disciplining them. By seeing the positive and remaining calm, these teachers maintained their emotional balance in difficult situations.

In addition to not judging students who were misbehaving, these teachers appeared not to hold grudges against students who had misbehaved. Students were disciplined and then the incident was forgotten. Students who had overstepped their boundaries did not have to earn the teacher's respect again. The teachers continued to show acceptance and positive regard for them. In return, students responded positively to the teacher's disciplinary request—lowering the potential stress of a stressful situation.

Tom provided a powerful example of a nonjudgmental attitude. He had a student who was showing up for class sporadically, whose behavior toward others was insensitive and disrespectful. Tom explained,

> I called him out in the hall on Friday and I said, "You know, I see a kid who isn't doing his work. He's kind of rude. He isn't really talking back a lot but he's not being real polite in class—a kid who's always run down and tired." And I said, "I'm concerned. I am not going to do a lot of prying but a lot of times if you tell me and let it out it will get better." And you could just see the tears going down. He just broke down big time, you know, at that point.

A similar example is provided by Dean, at Inner City High School. The vulnerable, high-risk student population Dean worked with would tax most teachers' patience. Dean explained that he tried to figure out the rationale behind the student's behavior and react to that, rather than judge the child. "I had this kid once in real trouble stand up, and I said, 'Man, you have got to start and get your book out!' He was like, 'No! No! F___ you! F___ you, man!' He was like screaming at me." Dean did not judge the student for his aberrant behavior, nor did he react to it. He understood something else had to be going on to cause such an intense reaction. He said, "Alright man, come on now. There is something up with you. Obviously you are angry about something else than this." Dean offered the student a private place to go so the student could calm down. When Dean spoke with the student a short time later he discovered that a family situation was upsetting the student. Calmer, the student broke down and cried as he shared the cause of his anger. (See Resource 14: Nonjudgmental Stance for brief examples.)

Quality Six: Sense of Humor

As mentioned earlier, these teachers were humorous and playful. Humor is defined as a quality that makes something laughable, amusing, or playful. Of course, the humor expressed by these teachers was not at the expense of others, but they often laughed at themselves. Lessons were presented with humor; students were motivated with humor; discipline was handled with humor; and classrooms were managed with humor. In fact, I would say that a couple of these teachers were just one step away from being standup comedians. They were fun to be around. They playfully teased students and students teased them. Tom said, "The students think I'm nuts, and that is great! I like the kids to laugh and I like them to joke around." Humor, when used good-naturedly like these teachers used it, helps communicate that we are accessible to others as well as alleviates our stress when in particularly tense situations.

As an example, Dale used a constant humorous banter to discipline, to instruct, to motivate, to acknowledge.

> Dale says, "Tell me why we are here." Students call out, "To learn math," "To get a credit," "Because you are such a cool guy." Dale says, "The reason we are here today is to learn percentages so that on the comp test we will see them and say POC—piece of cake." The class turns its attention on Dale. Dale grabs a student's notebook. He looks in the notebook and sees a sandwich. He examines the ham sandwich. "What percentage of this sandwich is bread and what percentage is filling?" The class rattles off different answers. Dale shows them—two-thirds bread, one-third filling. Amused, he says, "Maybe that's not true. There is a lot of mustard on this thing!" The students laugh.

When Pam was facilitating the debriefing on harassment, she flashed, "I feel like Oprah Winfrey!" Then she quickly proceeded into a short, impromptu vignette mimicking Oprah. She raced up and down the aisles, holding a make-believe microphone under the chins of different students, while she facetiously asked questions. (See Resource 15: Humor for brief examples.)

Quality Seven: Ability to Personally Detach

Detachment is the ability to acknowledge stressful events, but not to take personally the happenings surrounding stressful events. Individuals who are able to detach from stressful events of the day and keep a balanced perspective are less affected by their stressful work (Edelwich & Brodsky, 1980). Like a tolerance for ambiguity, detachment is a personal quality that is particularly hard to develop if we do not come by it naturally. Reasons for taking events personally are often seated in deeper psychological motives. But, as with tolerance for ambiguity, personal counseling can help if our individual efforts to learn to detach are not successful.

Detachment was a primary psychological coping mechanism for all the teachers. For instance, Dean said, "I am real good at detaching, as far as not taking it personally . . . This is part of life. You are going to have conflicts occur at our level [high school]. Just deal with it." Ruby and Dale had to learn to detach. Ruby says she used to want all the students to like her and was really upset when she had a conflict with a student. "Now I just have accepted that there are some kids that, for whatever reasons, are going to have personality conflicts with you, or they're not going to like the activities and things that you're doing, and that's okay." When asked about his strengths as a teacher, Dale mentions communication and detachment. "I've learned not to take everything personally. A lot of things are like water off a duck's back." All the observed teachers mentioned how much easier their jobs were when they detached from the stressful interactions.

Other evidence that demonstrated that these teachers detached is they did not assume responsibility for students' well-being. Even though they viewed nurturing students as an important way to accomplish their educational goals, they detached from the consequences of their efforts to connect with students. They did not have to be successful all the time. These teachers just did it, even if students chose to reject the teacher's efforts. They acknowledged that students who refused to respond to their nurturing efforts were difficult students to work with, but also they did not inappropriately assume responsibility for the decisions those students made. They just continued to reach out to students in the same manner, even though their nurturing efforts may have seemed in vain.

Summary of Personal Qualities for Connecting

The seven personal qualities and skills held in common by the teachers in my study enhance their ability to make healthy connections with students as well as alleviate the stress of their jobs. These personal qualities— genuineness and nonjudgmental attitude, tolerance for imperfection and ambiguity, sense of personal accountability, sense of humor, and the ability to detach—increase our ability to make healthy connections with students, and thus increase the sense of fulfillment and emotional rewards we get from our work. Although we may not come by all these personal qualities naturally, they are qualities we can nurture and develop within ourselves. These qualities will both help us reach our ultimate goal as a teacher—to make a difference for students—and keep us revitalized in the process.

INTERPERSONAL SKILLS THAT ENHANCE CONNECTING WITH STUDENTS

Besides the seven personal qualities discussed above, the teachers in my study held in common four interpersonal skills and relational resources:

1. Good interpersonal communication skills

2. Conflict resolution skills

3. Relational skills from positive childhood experiences

4. Skills at maintaining and utilizing a support system

Like the personal qualities, these skills and resources increase teachers' ability to reach their teaching goals. By doing so, these personal resources mediated the teachers' stress level, and helped them maintain their enthusiasm and professional energy.

Skill One: Interpersonal Communication Skills

Effective interpersonal communication skills are basic to the development and maintenance of healthy relationships (Johnson, 1972). Good communication skills are essential for successful conflict resolution or mediation. They are prerequisites to developing close and trusting relationships and thus crucial for making positive connections with students. If we would like to improve our ability to communicate—and make our jobs easier—these are skills readily taught through community colleges or at weekend workshops, and, with a little practice, are easy to apply.

All of the observed teachers valued and practiced good interpersonal communication skills such as listening, paraphrasing, summarizing, reflecting, and clarifying. These teachers valued listening and knew how important listening is for validating and making positive connections with students. They worked on their listening and paraphrasing skills. They practiced summarizing student comments to ensure they understood correctly. They reflected back to a student the question he or she asked, which allowed the student to hear his or her own question and to clarify his or her thinking. They checked their understanding with students to make sure they had heard the student's concern correctly. And they communicated responsively to student needs. (See Resource 16: Effective Communication Skills for brief examples.)

Skill Two: Conflict Resolution Skills

In order to maintain close, caring relationships, confidence in our ability to resolve conflict without damaging the relationship is imperative. Conflict resolution skills involve the ability to deal with intense emotional situations *as they occur*. With these skills we feel confident developing and maintaining close and caring relationships. We know we can handle conflict in a dignified and respectful manner; students know that conflict will be handled in a dignified and respectful manner. We are viewed as someone safe to get close to. The ability to resolve conflict eases our stress by giving us confidence in our ability to deal with any uncomfortable situation that may arise, as so often happens when working closely with others.

Conflict resolution strategies require a greater variety of communication skills than a regular conversation. Although the teachers' styles for resolving conflict differed, they were all confident in their ability to deal with tense and conflicting situations. Some of the observed teachers dealt with conflict by using mediating and negotiating strategies; others used diffusing strategies. Several of the observed teachers perceived themselves as key mediators for any conflict situation that arose within their buildings. For instance, at Inner City High School, Dean was often called on to break up fist fights, or to confiscate weapons from students. During three observation days alone, Dean was called out of the classroom to break up two arguments for other teachers. I was not able to observe these situations, but later learned from Dean that these were normal occurrences. Besides his communication skills, Dean had the advantage of his physical size and the respect he commanded on campus.

Pam's conflict resolution style emphasized listening and clarifying skills. She said,

> I firmly believe that most conflict is due to lack of communication, a lack of listening, or perceptions that differ. And so I try to make sure that the other people involved are listening to each other. If I'm one of them, then maybe I'm not listening to what this person is saying or maybe they're not listening to me. So I try to paraphrase, shift out of taking the situation personally.

In contrast, Dale dealt with conflict primarily by diffusing the situation. In fact, Dale said he often would let students be angry with him for a while because "at this age nine times out of ten they'll come back and just talk like nothing happened." Dale indicated that in really heated conflicts between a student and himself, he would send the student out for a while to give them both a chance to simmer down. Then he may ask a counselor to come assist with mediation of the conflict. Dale recognized that sometimes the student's anger was coming from places that he did not understand. The counselor helped him to see the source of the anger.

Not everyone is comfortable with conflict, but fortunately the skills to deal comfortably with conflict can be learned. Ruby stated that because of her abusive family background, conflict used to be difficult for her. But she has developed the communication and mediation skills to resolve conflicts with students or valued peers. When asked to describe how she handled a situation where there was conflict between herself and a student, Ruby said, "I deal with that student one-on-one and find out where the concern is, where the problem was, or where the lack of understanding was and try to paraphrase it and really focus in on where the lack of understanding came from and why." (See Resource 17: Conflict Resolution Skills.)

Skill Three: Relational Skills From Childhood Experiences

An often-overlooked but important personal resource affecting a teacher's ability to connect with students is the teacher's childhood experiences with bonding. Having positive bonding experiences with primary caregivers cultivates a natural ability to form positive connections with others as an adult (Bowlby, 1988; Main, Kaplan, & Cassidy, 1985). Positive experiences provide individuals with intrinsically healthy mental patterns for relating to others (Bowlby, 1988). Thus teachers who come from healthy, caring families find it easier to form close and caring connections with their students.

Four of the six teachers indicated they had happy, stable childhoods. Their family experiences were described as nurturing and supportive. When asked about their upbringing, they said such things as "I wouldn't trade [my childhood] for anything," and "I had a real nurturing upbringing. I had a real supportive mother and father and brothers and sister and we were all real tight." These teachers' families continue to be major sources of support and encouragement for them today, in addition to equipping them with healthy relational skills.

On the other side of the coin, psychological theorists contend that children raised with abusive parents tend to develop negative, unsuccessful patterns of relating. These negative patterns make it difficult to form healthy relationships as adults (Bowlby, 1988; Karen, 1990; Main et al., 1985). In other words, the skills for developing meaningful connections with others are passed from one generation to the next (Main et al., 1985).

Those of us who were reared in dysfunctional, abusive families, take heart. The good news is that psychological theorists also contend positive patterns for relating to others can be learned in cases where childhood bonding experiences were negative. A therapeutic intervention is necessary for us to work through these negative experiences (Main et al., 1985). In other words, teachers with childhood histories of chronic abuse may have difficulty forming healthy connections with their students without some type of therapeutic intervention resulting in personal insight and awareness. Besides not feeling competent to develop positive connections with their students, teachers from abusive families often find close relationships stressful. Without the social and emotional foundations and the resulting relational skills, the dynamics of a close personal connection become a personal burden (Bowlby, 1988). But, with just a little extra help, we all can develop the relational skills we need.

Two of the teachers in my study, Ruby and Pam, defined their families of origin as dysfunctional. In their families of origin there was physical and sexual abuse, abandonment, violent rage, and alcoholism. These teachers acknowledged that their parents did not provide them with an emotionally secure "base." Both Ruby and Pam, though, have been through intensive therapy to help them rework negative patterns for relating and integrate painful childhood experiences. Both teachers now are able to draw on their therapeutic experiences in ways that are helpful for developing meaningful connections with others. Their abusive family backgrounds and therapeutic experiences have become assets rather than liabilities. Both Ruby and Pam said that they would not be able to work with students the way they did if they had not gone to therapy.

Skill Four: Getting Support
From Family, Friends, and Professionals

Healthy relationships with family members not only equip us with healthy relational skills, they provide us with continual support and encouragement. Talking about stressful events with supportive family members, friends, and peers was another helpful coping technique used by these teachers. They turned to family, peers, and friends as sounding boards. All the teachers made reference to someone they trust with whom they can talk about the stresses of the day, and mentioned talking about difficult events as a technique to mediate stress. Tom described about how he learned to dialogue as an effective coping technique.

> I don't keep my feelings in like I used to. For a long time I think I fit the typical male stereotype of just holding everything in and not showing emotion. Things started to change when I was in my mid-twenties, I'd say, and I think today I talk a lot more. Sometimes it takes a little prodding still. I've got a wife who's pretty good at the prodding. She gets me to talk about it. So instead of bottling things in, I let things out.

Several teachers indicated that during really traumatic times, they sought professional assistance for sorting out their problems. One teacher mentioned that after being diagnosed with cancer several years earlier, she sought professional counseling to help her cope with the psychological aspects of the threatening disease while she underwent medical treatment. Another teacher mentioned seeking professional counseling to help her resolve some personal issues that were unnecessarily complicating her life as an adult. These teachers recognized that traumatic situations may be better handled by involving a professional than by depending on family and friends as confidantes, and they were willing to ask for professional assistance.

SUMMARY OF WHAT IT
TAKES TO REVITALIZE OURSELVES

The key to maintaining our professional energy is feeling confident in our ability to make a difference for students. When we highly value making a difference for students, knowing we *are* making that difference goes a long way toward sustaining our professional energy. We now know we can make a difference by developing close and caring connections with our students and becoming an adult who is meaningfully involved in their lives. The six observed teachers highlight for us distinct personal revitalization resources that helped them develop these caring relationships. These resources include (1) expansive beliefs about teaching; (2) personal qualities such as genuineness, nonjudgmental attitude, a tolerance for imperfection and ambiguity, a sense of accountability and humor, and an ability to detach; and (3) good interpersonal and relational skills.

Many of the personal qualities and interpersonal skills held in common by the six nurturing teachers are the same qualities and skills that counseling literature identifies as essential to be an effective counselor. In particular, the communication skills of listening, conflict resolution, and self-disclosure (Aspy & Roebuck, 1972; Wiggins, 1982) and the personal qualities of genuineness, nonjudgmental attitude, and good interpersonal skills (Carkhuff, 1969, 1987; Rogers, Gendlin, Keisler, & Truax, 1967; Small, 1981) have been identified for effective helping. Just as these qualities and skills are developed in individuals who want to be counselors or effective helpers, they can be developed and refined in teachers (Mendes, 2003). It appears that if we develop these personal revitalizing resources, a job that, for some teachers, requires too intense an investment for too little reward becomes a source of emotional rewards and personal satisfaction.

5

Yeah, I Hear You, But . . .

Jim is the father of one of Tom's troubled students. I phone Jim and his wife to ask permission to interview their son. I can tell by the tone of the telephone conversation that they are concerned about their son, Jerry, and want what is best for him. Jerry has been skipping school and is delinquent with his schoolwork. His attitude seems indifferent and apathetic, and his grades reflect his apparent lack of interest in school. Although Jerry seems to be making a turnaround in behavior, Jim and his wife are still worried about their son's low self-esteem.

During the phone conversation, it is clear that Jim has been reflecting on his role in his son's difficulties at school. He confides in me that he was raised in an orphanage, which has affected his parenting skills.

"I made a commitment to myself that when I had kids, I would give them everything. I would do everything for my kids. I now realize that alone I cannot give my sons everything they need to grow up to be happy and well-adjusted. That was a hard lesson for me to learn."

Jim continues, "Jerry entered Suburb Junior High this fall with little interest in school. There are a couple of teachers there, though, that have been a big help to him. He seems to have really connected with them and they are helping him. Tom is one of them. Tom has made a big impact on Jerry. He gives him second chances, encouragement, and support, and I see Jerry's self-esteem shooting up. I'm really thankful for the role Tom's playing in Jerry's life." Jim hesitates for a moment, then adds, "I would've liked to have done it all by myself, but I know now I need other people, as well as me, to direct his life."

Jim chats with me a little longer about the valuable help Suburb Junior High teachers are providing him in shaping a more positive attitude toward life with his son. Then he comments again on Tom. "You know, with all Tom does for his students, he never crosses the line of being a parent to his students. He doesn't take over my role. He clearly stays in his role as a teacher. I admire that."

THE GOOD NEWS

The good news is we do make a difference for our students. The most powerful and effective way we help students overcome all the negative influences in their environment is by developing close and caring relationships with them. Research shows our relationship with our students is *key*. By just doing our jobs the best we can, and making a special effort to connect with each child, we *can* change the course of a child's life. We do not need to get involved in more committee assignments or add other responsibilities to our busy schedules. We do not have to become surrogate parents, social workers, or counselors. We simply need to reach out to our students and make healthy, meaningful connections with them.

We are caring teachers. Knowing how we relate to students is *the* most powerful tool we have for making a difference in their lives. It gives us inspiration and a sense of purpose in our efforts to develop caring connections. We now understand that the heart of caring in a teacher-student relationship is found in respect. Through the exemplars provided, we were able to vicariously watch six teachers successfully make healthy connections with their students during their daily routines. The examples and vivid descriptions provided us with a variety of caring behaviors. Although there are probably many other ways for teachers to develop healthy relationships with students, we are now familiar with several role-appropriate ways for nurturing close and caring connections with students. Caring behavior requires nothing extraordinary from us, except that we do our jobs well.

YES, BUT . . .

For some teachers, the information and insights gleaned from this book affirm and make sense of what they are already doing. For other teachers, this information may serve to encourage them to try some new behaviors. Even so, many of us may still have valid concerns, which create uncertainty and hesitation when we consider changing our approach to teaching in the direction this book advocates. Because I have spoken with many teachers from various districts about my study, I have identified some major common concerns teachers have about forming close and caring relationships with students.

RESPONDING TO CONCERNS

- **I became a teacher to teach, not to promote student social and emotional development. I don't believe nurturing students' personal growth is part of my job.**

It's true that not all of us enter the teaching profession with the goal of promoting the personal growth of our students, especially those of us who are secondary school teachers. Many of us are content specialists. We love our subjects. We became teachers because we wanted to inspire others to love it also. Traditionally, teachers are viewed as responsible only for the cognitive development or academic outcomes of students. We are not viewed as responsible for students' social and emotional development. If you do not believe promoting student personal growth is part of your job, you need only to reframe this responsibility and think of developing good strong connections with your students. Making healthy connections with students *is* a traditional responsibility of teachers. Healthy teacher-student relationships are an essential component of a teacher's job and promote student learning (Goodman, Sutton, & Harkavy, 1995; O'Donnell et al., 1992). As Noblit, Rogers, and McCadden (1995) say, "without this connection, teachers may have the subject-matter knowledge, and the technical ability to teach, but the opportunities for real learning will be scarce, because what the teacher does not have is the student" (p. 683). *You don't need to focus on the personal growth of your students as an educational goal; you can just focus on making healthy connections with students as a means of enhancing student comprehension of the subject you love, and the growth will take care of itself.*

- **I want to make a difference in student lives, but I don't see myself as a nurturing person. Is there something I can do?**

Pam, the social studies teacher at Suburban Junior High, once said to me, "You know, I never really considered myself a very nurturing teacher until you showed up. I never thought of it one way or another. So I'm just really surprised that you would even want to talk to me about this stuff!" I probed her a little further: "What is your image of a nurturing teacher?" She responded, "I don't know." Then after a pause she said, "I get this feeling . . . like my kindergarten teacher was real nurturing." She laughed as she reminisced. "She used to feed us cookies and we'd have naps. That's what I think of when I think of nurturing . . . like a mom, you know." Pam laughed again, paused, and then quickly added, "I mean, I'm not like these kids' mother. I mean, I get the image of this kind of round, gray-haired matron, right? . . . who always smells like fresh baked bread or something."

We all have our personal impressions and beliefs about behaviors that are nurturing, and these beliefs shape our thinking about the subject. Pam did not see herself as nurturing. To her, a teacher needed to be "mothering" the students to be nurturing. The information and insights provided by this study help us get beyond our preconceived notions about nurturing. They give us different ways to think about what nurtures students in the caring teacher-student relationship.

The fact that six teachers with very different personalities had very different styles for making caring connections with students helps discount some common misconceptions about a teacher's caring behavior. First, caring does not require us to be affectionate, sweet, gentle, and warm. Several of the teachers in the study demonstrated that we can nurture when being cool and professionally detached. Touching students, although helpful, is not necessary either. In fact, several of the teachers studied *avoided* touching. Second, caring is not gender dependent. It is easy to assume that women can nurture more effectively than men. This study demonstrates that male teachers can nurture as well as female teachers. Third, caring is not synonymous with permissiveness. Some people believe that when we are caring toward students we are indulgent and lenient, or that caring is associated with weakness or permissiveness. The nurturing teachers in the book demonstrate one can nurture *and* be a strict disciplinarian. *The bottom line for a teacher's behavior to be caring appears to be treating students with dignity and respect. If you treat students respectfully, listen to them, and keep their confidence, they perceive you as caring.*

• **I don't feel comfortable getting as involved with students as the teachers do in this book. What can I do without getting so involved and still get positive results?**

If you do not want to become involved to the degree of, let's say, Dean or Gail, just treating students with dignity and respect will make a difference. Any interaction with students in which a teacher treats students with dignity and respect will get positive results. Recall Tom's story at the beginning of Chapter 2 regarding the teacher who made the difference in his life. When Tom was a student in high school, he was using drugs and involved in activities he should not have been. It was his literature teacher, Mr. M___, who helped turn Tom around. Mr. M___ was a "geek." He was not a star. He was not athletic. He didn't socialize with the students. He wasn't even a "favorite" teacher of the students. In fact, Tom said some students made fun of him. But students all knew he cared. How? He showed respect for them. In class, Mr. M___ sought their opinions and ideas, he valued their thoughts, and he demonstrated he believed in his students' capabilities. This recognition alone was enough to make a powerful difference for Tom. Tom credits Mr. M___ with his life.

Students don't necessarily need adults to be intimately involved with them or spend a lot of time with them. They need adults who care about them and respect them. *What you can do to get positive results is to treat your students respectfully by listening to them, knowing their names, talking with them, soliciting their opinions, valuing their ideas, and believing they are capable. And when they need correction or guidance, respectfully showing them their mistakes only provides additional opportunities to learn and develop the skills necessary to be productive, successful adults.*

- **If I am always nurturing, don't I run the risk of giving up some of my control as a teacher?**

The fear of losing one's control as a teacher is a common concern. If we associate caring behavior with being weak and indulgent (Weinstein, 1998), we will fear losing our ability to maintain control of our classrooms. With this misconception, nurturing students is often associated with loss of our power as teachers.

The caring teachers described in this book demonstrate caring can *increase* a teacher's power. The teachers in this little book all had tight control over their classrooms because students treated them respectfully. Three of the teachers were described as strict by their students, and yet these teachers still clearly communicated caring to their students. Two teachers identified themselves as permissive; they could tolerate a high level of disruption before their patience was tried. But when they disciplined they were committed to firmness and consistency and, of course, respectfulness. Interestingly, the students of these two teachers did not see them as permissive. Their students described them as tolerant and understanding, yet firm disciplinarians.

Understanding the power base from which the observed teachers worked helps explain why they did not lose power by being consistently caring. These teachers were not dependent on the legitimate power granted to them by virtue of their position as teachers. Nor did they motivate behavioral change by dangling possible rewards or threatening punishment. The source of power for these teachers was a student's admiration and respect for them. This power base is called referent power (French & Raven, 1959). With referent power, students frequently identify with the teacher as a role model. And they are willing to adjust their behavior so as not to lose the love and respect of the teacher who carries referent power.

Referent power is often associated with teacher charisma, but it can be developed by most teachers. How? By treating students with dignity and respect. Referent power is the most influential source of power we have (French & Raven, 1959). Referent power is used caringly and respectfully *in service* of students. No, we do not lose power when assuming a nurturing posture with students; we gain it. In fact, how we wield our power while in our teaching role may be the key to our ability to make a difference in student lives. *The respectful and caring use of a teacher's power seems quintessential to developing close and trusting relationships with students.*

- **What about students who resist caring or respond negatively? How do resistant students affect my ability to nurture students?**

No doubt student receptivity affects a teacher's capacity to make healthy connections. In this study, several of the teachers mentioned that some of their students appeared indifferent or unaffected by the concern and care they were shown. These teachers indicated that they just continued to nurture, whether or not students were receptive.

The teachers in this study nurtured students because it was what *they* wanted to do, not because it was what students wanted or needed, necessarily. Whether or not a student responds is really inconsequential to whether we should continue caring or not. Knowing the personal beliefs that motivate these teachers to care for students, nurturing for nurturing's sake despite student response makes sense. Eventually some resistant students come around and respond to the teacher's caring, as a student in Pam's class indicated. "At the beginning of the year, I didn't like her and I didn't want to be in her class. Now, I'm glad that I have her for my social studies teacher and I want to get her again next year." And some students may never come around.

Looking at this question from another perspective, one way resistant students really impose on a teacher's capacity to care is by becoming an emotional drain. Burnout is associated with giving more than one receives. If we are working in an environment where a lot of students are nonreceptive to our efforts to make meaningful connections, then burnout is imminent—unless our work environment provides other kudos. It would be difficult for us to maintain our professional energy and an intense level of caring and involvement in an environment where there is little acknowledgment of our efforts. So, practically speaking, how realistic is it for teachers whose primary educational goal is student growth to stay in work environments where we get few rewards for our sincere efforts? We need to find school environments that support our efforts. *So keep nurturing, because it is the thing you want to do, it is the right thing to do, and eventually some resistant students will come around and thank you. But to avoid burnout, make sure your colleagues, principal, and work environment nurture you too.*

- **Not all students respond equally to nurturing. How can I avoid playing favorites?**

Students have varying degrees of relational skills. Understandably, it is easier for us to respond and nurture students who are receptive. When students are nonresponsive to our sincere efforts, it may be difficult not to ignore them. Interestingly, some students from the study talked about one of the observed teachers playing favorites. When I asked, "Does she treat all students the same?" the student's response was enlightening. "No . . . I mean I think every teacher has favorites. She gives a little extra to everybody . . . she tries to spread it out. Sometimes, though, she gives more to some than others. But life isn't fair. Sometimes you get lucky or whatever." Such wisdom from the mouths of babes! It is true. *Life does not treat us all equally. We must learn to make the most of the hand we are dealt. In the real world, students are going to have to learn to work with preferential treatment. Without a doubt, we should try our best to not play favorites, and we should recognize we are human when we do.*

- **Do all teachers need to become caring? Does the information about these six teachers apply to all of us?**

Although we may not be exactly like any of the teachers described, we can adapt and adjust the principles described to fit our style. But is it necessary for all teachers to become caring?

Dean's thinking on this question shifted my thoughts greatly on this topic. Dean pointed out that when students graduate into the work world they are not surrounded by bosses and colleagues who all reach out and nurture them. Students need to learn to get along with all types of people—difficult people, people they hate, people with all types of preferential treatment—in order to be successful in this world. So, in reality, it *is* best for students *not* to have every teacher a nurturing teacher. As Dean said, "That's why I never dog a teacher for style!" I felt more hopeful recognizing the truth in what Dean said. Not all teachers need to choose to nurture.

JUST LIKE YOU OR ME

I find it reassuring to remember that the six observed teachers were not superstars; they were singular individuals who were dedicated and motivated to help young people—just like you or me. They had some common personality traits, but they were also different in many ways. Some of these teachers were strict, detached, and almost cool toward students; others were warm, compassionate, and easygoing. They used a variety of different strategies to facilitate caring connections with students. Some held high expectations for student performance; others pushed for motivation in learning but felt rewarded when students simply attended class and were respectful. Some teachers used self-disclosure; others remained private about their personal lives. These teachers also exhibited a wide variety of styles for teaching and disciplining. Some used traditional lecture modes for curriculum delivery; others used cooperative learning or group strategies. They exhibited different tolerances for classroom noise. Some had classrooms that were rowdy; others had classrooms in which you could hear a pin drop.

In spite of all these differences, the teachers developed healthy emotional connections with their students. They all earned the respect of their students. The core underlying behavioral response or attitude they held in common was respectful treatment of students, which is applicable to all teachers. *We can all treat students with dignity and respect; in fact we should treat all people with dignity and respect.*

SOME CONCLUDING THOUGHTS

The real message of my research is that for teachers to make a difference in student lives we do not need budget increases, radical restructuring, federal mandates, or changes in our school policies. Rather, all we may need is subtle changes in our attitudes and behaviors so that we consciously build a caring, respectful culture. The relationship between teacher and students is often overlooked when discussing school restructuring and reform, *yet it is key*. As Maguire said, "If the relationships are wrong between teachers and students, for whatever reasons, you can restructure until the cows come home, but transformation won't take place" (Rothman, 1992, p. 1). Our role in our students' lives *is* powerful.

It was an awe-inspiring experience to observe these six teachers working to maintain healthy caring relationships with students. To the teachers in this study, it was just their jobs. To their students, it may have been their lifeline. Teachers have no way of knowing the impact they are making on the future. Not many of us, as mature adults, take the time to go back and acknowledge the teacher who made a difference for us. But after meeting these teachers, many of you may be inspired, as I was, to make contact with the teacher who made a difference for you.

And for those of us who choose to reach out to our students, although we have no way of knowing how many individuals we have redirected to become productive and successful citizens, we can acknowledge that we are doing good. The teachers in my study represent a whole cadre of teachers who are making a difference in young people's lives. As Kidder (1990) so aptly stated in his book, *Among School Children:*

> Good teachers put snags in the river of children passing by, and over the years, they redirect hundreds of lives. Many people find it easy to imagine unseen webs of malevolent conspiracy in the world, and they are not always wrong. But there is also an innocence that conspires to hold humanity together, and it is made of people who can never fully know the good they have done. (p. 313)

I hope this little book gives you just the inspiration and assurance you need to continue teaching for another twenty years.

Resources:

Supporting Data From Each Teacher

Resource 1

Discipline as Moral Guidance

Dale: One student, Bill, a troublemaker, comes up behind Dale and puts his paper on Dale's back and starts to sign it. Dale says, "Don't write on my back. There are plenty of desks around here to write on." Bill tries to jive with him by saying, "Shut up, man." Dale smiles, looks him directly in the eyes, and says, "What happens to you when you say that to your Dad?" Bill stops and says, "He pops me." Dale quietly quizzes the student, "Maybe I should pop you?" Bill looks apologetic. He then continues more appropriate social banter with Dale. Dale immediately joins in as if nothing had happened. Within minutes, Dale is teasing Bill about greasing his hair. Bill and the students laugh.

Dean: Dean tells his student assistant, "Hey, you know what? We need to clean this fish tank up." She says, "Oh no! I'm not going to do that. You are the one who killed the fish." Dean says gently, "I want you to empty the water out of there into the sink." She says, "I am not going to stick my hands into that water with all those dead fish!" Ignoring what she just said, Dean says in a light tone, "I want you to do this." He demonstrates how she is to take a container and transfer the water out of the tank to the sink. She says again, "I am not going to stick my hands into that water." Dean responds, "Then go to the nurse's station and get some rubber gloves." She retorts, "The nurse is never there when I go down there." Dean calmly replies, "Then I will go with you to get the gloves because this is your job and I want you to do it. This is your responsibility." Dean and the student leave the room for the nurse's station.

Gail: Gail walks around the room in between the desks, watching how people are working. She stops at one of the clusters and gently says to a female student wearing a beautiful new parka, "How did you get that coat?" The female student looks up and says, "It was on sale." Gail softly says, "Take it back." The female students asks, "Why?" Gail says, "You don't keep what you can't pay for." The student was numbly quiet. Gail moves on without another word.

Pam: Pam is working in a simulated archaeological dig with the students huddled around her. Someone says, "This sucks." Pam looks up and says quietly, "Who said that?" The culprit immediately identifies himself. She asks him to step outside. After the demonstration, Pam steps outside with the student for a moment. She asks him if he knows why he was sent out of class. "Yes, I was disrespectful." She says, "Do you have anything to say to me?" He says "I am sorry" and they enter the room together.

Ruby: One small group of boys are kidding around and one student says, "Oh shit." (Swearing is not acceptable behavior in Ruby's classroom.) Ruby says calmly to the student, "Carl, see me after class." Carl turns to his friends and says, "I said shoot." His friend slowly shakes his head no. Carl meekly says, "Ship?" The class laughs and so does Ruby. After class, Ruby reminds Carl of the class rule about swearing.

Resource 2

Treating Students With Dignity and Respect

Dale: Dale addresses the students as "ladies and gentlemen." "Ladies and gentlemen, I am glad to see you. I am really glad to see you. We need paper, pencils, and books today."

     When talking about experiences from his high school years that influenced who he is today, Dales says, "The only thing I really carry with me [is] treat the kids with respect. I tell them at the first of the year, I say, I'm going to earn your respect. I'm going to work really hard to earn your respect. And I will respect you just as much as you respect me."

Dean: In talking to Dean at lunch, he says, "These kids are adults. They've already made more decisions in their life than you or I have had to. You can't treat them like kids, but like adults. Take for instance the kid sitting up there studying. [Dean points to a small boy quietly studying.] He's a gang member and has been faced with situations you or I have not dreamed of." Surprised, I comment on how small he is to be a gang member. Dean says, "The gun is the equalizer."

Gail: When asked what she assessed as her strength as a teacher, Gail says, "My ability to empathize with the students, to put myself in their place. . . . I see them as little people. I see them as independent thinkers, as very nice people. Even the ones who are sort of rough. They are really nice but you have to cut through the roughness to get to the nice part. I think I have the ability to cut through the edges and get through to the nice person, or at least find out what's wrong, what's going on in that person's life that perhaps has made that person what society perceives as a mean person or a bad person."

     Gail calls students up to the lectern to talk to them individually. When asked what she says to students, she responds, "It is usually something that you don't want to say out loud in front of students. Even praise—some students don't like you to praise them in front of their friends because they will be seen as teacher's pet. So I kind of do it quietly."

Pam: When asked what are the qualities of a healthy, caring relationship between a teacher and a student, Pam responds, "One is mutual respect. Another is clear boundaries. Another is clear expectations and clear consequences. That's pretty easy, huh?

"I relate to them as people. . . . I don't talk down to kids. I never have, I don't think, you know, in a condescending way. 'Oh, this is a child who wouldn't understand.' I expect kids to understand the question and be able to communicate with me—their needs and wants and that kind of thing.

"I don't speak in a different language. I never talk down to them. I use words that sometimes I know they don't know the meaning of. And I try to either have them work it out in context or if someone asks me, I have them look it up. It's like I don't alter how I speak to these guys."

Ruby: One of the ground rules for teacher and student behavior in Ruby's class is respect. "I think we have four of them [ground rules]: respect, set a goal, think positive, and make up work. I think those are the four posted up there."

Ruby suggests that students get up and move around to exchange their strength inventory with other students. Two students don't get up. She says, "Don't you guys get tired of sitting all day long?" They answer, "No." She says, "That is amazing. When I am in meetings all day, I get real tired of sitting." They answer, "Yes, but we are used to it. You are not because you are standing most of the time." Ruby pauses. "Well, that is right," she says. She allows them to remain in their seats.

"I do my very best to never confront kids in front of other kids if it's a thing where I have to get on them about their behavior. So a lot of times I'll take the two kids outside."

Tom: Tom addresses the boys as "sirs" and the girls as "ladies." One student responded, "We treat him with respect because he treats us with respect."

The student teacher says, "I think it comes down to respect. There is a definite two-way respect in that classroom. You know, a lot of teachers expect the kids to respect them, but it's not reciprocated."

Resource 3

Creating a Safe Learning Environment

Dale: "I call [students] by name or give them some kind of individual attention. I'm trying to get them to have confidence in me so they can ask me a question. A lot of kids seem embarrassed to ask questions. So I'm trying to eliminate that feeling so they can ask me about anything and feel real comfortable."

Data from in-class observations: Dale chats with the students while they work on their homework. He seems to just accept everyone as equals, treating everyone in the same relaxed, good-natured manner. Students may start talking about something, and Dale joins in and shares in the fun. . . . It is a very comfortable and low-key class. Students appear to be free to talk to him about almost anything, from the trouble they got into over the weekend to getting detention for passing gas in another teacher's class.

Danny, a student with a learning disability, says, "[Dale] stays calm all the time. . . . I have never, never, heard him yell."

Dean: Rosie, when asked what Dean does that makes him such a caring teacher, said, "Well, just the way he acts. I mean, he's always making sure everything is okay, making sure you do your work, and he makes you feel really good if you do your work."

Data from in-class observations: He creates an incredible space for students to be themselves. Dean always uses a soft voice. During the whole day, I never heard him raise his voice to quiet the group or redirect their behavior. Even though less playful than the last time I observed him, he was always calm in voice. When lecturing, he often reflects questions back to the group. . . . He seldom rejects an answer entirely but rather says, "a little like that" or "almost, but what about this?"

Gail: When Gail was asked for the qualities of a healthy, caring relationship with students, the quality she mentioned was providing a safe environment. "I guess . . . their knowing that they can come and talk to me just about . . . anything. I'm not going to get mad at them or judge them."

Data from in-class observations: Gail's curriculum is relevant to the African American and minority cultures. Each day I entered the classroom, students were working with material that was relevant to their culture. For instance, the first day students were reading a book titled *Farewell to Manzanar*, about an Asian American family. The second day they were studying Martin Luther King, Jr.'s speech, "I Have a Dream." The third day students were reading *The Life You Save*, a play about African Americans written in African American dialect.

Pam: "Why do people try to sidestep responsibility? They do it because they're afraid. If you remove fear, then you're taking a huge amount of anxiety off of kids. You know, I am not going to yell at them. I'm not going to belittle them. I'm not going to ridicule them. I'm not going to embarrass them. I just want them to self-correct and they know that."

Data from in-class observations: When students forgot to bring from home items to simulate an archaeological dig, Pam had them brainstorm in teams a plan to ensure that they would remember to bring all the items for the assignment to class the next day. Pam did not criticize, nag, or tell them what they had better do to make sure the items were here the next day.

Ruby: "I want kids to feel okay to talk to me. Within the realm of the health class, we talk abut so many issues in there. I guess I want them to feel safe if we're going to do a writing assignment and they're going to talk about particular issues that relate to teens. I want them to feel safe if they want to write that they've experienced something . . . I just let them know that it remains confidential between us."

Data from in-class observations: Ruby had given students the assignment of creating a 2′ × 3′ personal collage by creatively using clippings from magazines to depict who they are. She asked the group, "What do you think that I will not let you put on the collage?" A student says, "Tobacco and alcohol." Ruby pauses and says, "Other students also have thought that I would not permit alcohol and tobacco, but I have let students do that because if alcohol and tobacco are really that important to them, they need to express that." Another student says, "Sick!" Ruby pauses and says, "How else can we say we don't approve without putting people down?" They talk a little about this idea. She explains that "people need to feel free to express who they are . . . and that is where their lives are at." She goes on to define the guidelines as no pictures of nudity, no profanity, and no put-downs of other people.

Tom: "They generally feel pretty comfortable in here. I mean by the way they act and talk and do everything else in here. The fact that we had 81 out of 85 kids choose to come back to team-taught courses this year."

Data from in-class observations: Tom laughs and jokes with them when they make a mistake. Students are not afraid to toss out an answer. They try but are not afraid to make a mistake. They readily acknowledge when they don't know. In observing Tom's class, I was not concerned that he would shame and criticize students. I was not anticipating abrupt, angry words. Students do not hesitate to admit when they have misbehaved.

Data from student teacher: [The student teacher describes student behavior after a particularly rowdy day when a substitute teacher was there.] Tom said, "I heard there were some problems yesterday. What were they?" And they immediately confessed, and it wasn't Jimmy telling on Susie and Susie telling on Bobby. The kids who had been the problem children said, "I did this." That right there showed me they have a whole heck of a lot of respect for him because when they were caught they didn't try to weasel out of it. . . . They didn't try, "Well, I did it because" or whatever it was. They just said, "I did this." Tom's response was, "We don't do that." [Then Tom had the student teacher share how he felt watching the kids behave as they did from the back of the room.] "I think he let them 'guilt trip' themselves."

Resource 4

Student Recognition of and Reaction to Respectful Treatment

Dale: I commented to a student that when Dale disciplines, students seem to adjust their behavior without grumbling or resistance. The student's response was, "Because he gives us a lot, and I think the students know that we owe him at least our attention."

    Annette knows Dale sees her as a resource rather than an object. She says, "Some teachers think 'I'm the boss and you're the student and no matter what you say you're wrong and I'm right.' . . . You can't connect because you feel like they're superior to you. [Dale] has always told us that teachers and students are the same and to learn from the students because they can teach you things too."

    Annette feels respected. "After being suspended for a while, you come back and it's like totally weird being in school again. And you know, I walked in [Dale's] classroom and he's like, 'Hey Annette! You're back! Congratulations, you made it!' You know, he is like, 'Have a seat. Come on. We're waiting for you' and stuff. You know, he like welcomed me." Annette admits trying harder and doing better in Dale's classes. "I mean, he's the only math teacher I've learned from. I'm good at math but I usually don't get good grades in it. All my life I've gotten D's and stuff, and this year I'm finally getting Bs in his class."

Dean: "Well, everyone respects him. Like if people don't respect you, the teacher, and the teacher tells them to do [something], they'll just talk back and then the teacher will have to make them leave or something. And the people won't care. But people don't really like it when [Dean] gets mad at them, I don't think."

    "Just when he tells you, people got enough respect for him just to quit, to stop doing it right when he says it."

Gail: When asked how he thought Gail saw him as a student, Jake replies, "I think she respects me as a leader . . . because she asks me a lot for opinions and advice. Sometimes she has me help other people because she knows I'm capable of believing in them and responsible enough to help them without screwing around." Jake believes another teacher whom Jake does not like sees him as "irresponsible and not willing to do his work" because that is the way Jake treats his class.

Pam: "She doesn't really have to do a lot of discipline in our class because I'm pretty sure that our whole class loves her, you know."

After describing how much fun it was to cause trouble in a class of a teacher he doesn't respect, Rick says, "I don't really like to get into trouble in [Pam's] class, really. I'm not really trying for it [to get into trouble as in other classes]. I don't like to deal with getting in trouble in her class."

Ruby: When talking about a teacher she does not like, Sally believes this teacher would describe her as "a kind person but not willing to respect [the teacher] and not willing to do as much work and stuff as she would like me to do." Sally is a good student in Ruby's class. Sally says, "[Ruby] is a really caring teacher and she is a lot better than all the other teachers. And it's not just carping; it's about the teaching too. She's a really good teacher. She makes it where you learn something and you always will have it."

Peter knows that he is more than a job to Ruby. "She seems to enjoy being here. I think she would probably still do this job if she wasn't getting paid. I think she likes it enough that she'd do that."

Tom: "We treat him with respect because he treats us with respect."

"He just takes a special interest in each one of the students. He tries to help each one of them. . . . He treats everybody fair. [He] tries to be fair with everybody. . . . I think everybody in our class knows that he could be strict but he's just nice to us, so I think that's why everybody's nice back to him."

"He doesn't have to threaten. He doesn't have to yell and scream. He doesn't have to do anything. I think it comes down to respect. There is a definite two-way respect in [Tom's] classroom. You know, a lot of teachers expect the kids to respect them, but it's not reciprocated. . . . He treats them like they're young adults, to a certain extent."

Resource 5

Student Receptiveness to and Perception of a Teacher's Caring

Dale: "He understands, you know, that we're teenagers and stuff. And he just cares. I don't know why, you know, he doesn't really have a reason to, I guess. But he just does. He shows it to us by, you know, he makes it a point to talk to us before class starts and after class ends. And it's not just like math for him. It's life and math put together."

"He's the kind of person where, you know, that if you tell him something he's not going to tell it to everybody."

When asked what he would tell student teachers on how to develop a close and trusting relationship with students, Danny responded, "Stay in [Dale's] classroom for a bit and watch him work."

Dean: "He cares about all the kids, not only the ones he knows. He cares about all the kids. So it's like if anybody has a problem, usually they'll go to [Dean] and [he] will then try to help them out."

"He's just . . . he's there if you need something. He knows how to make time. If he can't talk to you in school, during class, he'll like come back after school. He's always there."

Gail: "One quality that I see is that she is a caring person. She cares a lot about kids."

"She's easy to talk to. She tries to understand your problems. She jokes with you. She's just . . . she's open. You can talk to her and that's the teacher who cares."

When asked what makes Gail a caring teacher, Susan responded, "[Other teachers] don't ask you, like, if you're having a bad day. They don't ask you if you're okay or anything like that. It's like . . . I'll tell her such and such is happening and I'm really worried and she'll tell me . . . The other teachers just don't ask."

Pam: "Well, there are teachers that will always say, 'If you have a problem you can come to me' but you never really go to them. . . . I knew it was all right to talk [to Pam] about . . . my things, about my friends and stuff like that and she's really caring."

Rick was in some serious trouble at school. "Like, I had this thing going on with the school and stuff, and this one girl thought we did something but we didn't do any of it. Me and my friends . . . we really didn't. I didn't want to talk to the counselor because the counselor was, like, all on their side and so he wouldn't even listen to us. So then [Pam] said I could talk to her and then I just went and talked to her."

"Well, like, she'll let you talk about [stuff]. If you have any problems, she'll talk about it with you. I think everyone likes [Pam] except people like [names a student]. He has, like, an attitude toward [to Pam]."

Ruby: "The way she talks and the way she's really caring. Just the way she goes out of her way to get to know some people. . . . She kind of lets you know that she is there to listen to you and she's just, like, a real sweet person and she goes out of her way to get to know kids. . . . Just that I really like her a lot and that she's just a really caring teacher."

"She just [holds] out her arms. If you ever wanted to talk to anybody, whenever you wanted to. She's always there for you. She's pretty cool. She gives you good advice . . . the different choices that you could make. Like . . . she's just really cool. Always there when you need her."

Tom: "He's talked to me a few times. When he found out that I can't talk to my parents, he gave us a counselor that he used to go to that we went to. . . . He takes a special interest in each one of his students. He tries to help each one of them."

"He's nice and he'll listen to you if you have anything to say. He's honest."

When Jerry was asked what he would tell other students who were planning to take Tom's class, he responded, "I would tell them that he's a nice guy. He has homework, lots of homework that's sort of simple, but you have to think a little harder than you would in a regular social studies class . . . all I know is that he's a real nice guy that someone can trust."

Resource 6

Commitment to Student Learning

Dale: Dale described a time he negotiated with a student to motivate her to study her math. "I said, 'Andrea, I will buy you a tank of gas if you pass the comp test . . . and you can buy me a tank of gas if you don't.' Well, she did not pass the comp test, and I could have gone back and said, 'You really owe me that tank of gas.' But no, I didn't care if I ever collected that. I would rather have her just pass that comp test."

Dean: During one classroom observation, I observed Dean working really hard to get students motivated for a test. During the last seven minutes of class, students were coming up to Dean's desk and double-checking their grades. The upcoming test was the final test. Dean kept dogging the students to do better. One student, Steve, went up after class. Dean said, "If I am dogging you, it is because I care about you and I don't want you to fail."

Gail: "Right now I've kind of geared my language arts courses toward project-based and performance-based and student outcome, even in lieu of a written test. We have a lot of written work projects, so I can see exactly what the students have gotten from either the literature or some sort of assignment. They have a portfolio when they leave the classroom. So they get to look at it and say, 'This is what I have learned and this is how I understood the lesson or what it means to me.' And they get to see, they hold in their hands what they understand."

Pam: "I try real hard to be clear about what I expect, what the limits are, and what consequences there will be if those expectations are not met. I do the assignments myself before I have them do them so I know what to expect. Nothing is worse than having a teacher give you an assignment that is undoable for some reason. Like maybe your library doesn't have the resources to complete the assignment and you're just stymied. Well, an eighth grader just says, 'Well, forget it. I'm just not going to do anything.' They might not communicate to the teacher that it's because they didn't have the right resources . . . so my practice is to read the lessons that I'm having them read. And I answer the questions so I know where and how it's phrased in the book. When they say, 'It doesn't exist,' it's like, okay, try this, because I've done it. I know. I've been through the process. It takes time to do that but it pays off, it really pays off."

Ruby: "I am knowledgeable about what it is that I teach. And you know, if there's something I don't know when a kid asks me, I'll get back to them. And I don't have any problem saying 'I don't know this but I'll find out and get back to you.' I think I really believe in the whole process of education. I believe it's important for kids to be here and I believe it's important for them to be taking the class that I'm fortunate to be teaching."

Tom: "I was honest with [the students], told them this is the way it's going to be and I know you can do it. And I had high expectations. And my part of the contract was I agreed to create an individual educational plan for the kids, devote time outside of school to make sure that they were able to get done if they needed any extra help, and at any point in time be there as their mentor in terms of working with the teachers at school other than me that they have to deal with."

Resource 7

Personal Motivation to Be a Teacher

Dale: When asked what attracted him to the teaching profession, Dale answered, "See, I was a baseball player and I wanted to stay involved with the sport or just coaching in general. I thought maybe physical therapy. As I got into it, I found out I wasn't really a guy for all the muscles and all of that stuff. . . . I thought, 'I can coach if I can get into the teaching end.' As I got into education, I found I was really comfortable. I felt good about myself when people learned things. I seemed to put people at ease and have them feel good about math. I did not want to be a PE teacher because I wanted to be challenged. . . . Anyone I figured could, hey, throw the balls out and have fun. But this was the ticket for me—still being able to be involved in sports and able to help kids."

Dean: "I had teachers at my high school who were with me. They really stuck with me. They understood a lot of times—sometimes they did not understand but they were always there for me. . . . And so as I went through life I realized, you know something, I would like to help others like they helped me. Maybe I could actually give some [of what they gave me] back.

"Those kids are my clients. Those kids are my people whom I am serving. I got to look at their needs. I got to react to their needs. What is best for them? Everything that I do in my heart it is like, 'What is best for them?'"

Gail: When asked about her purpose as a teacher, Gail responded, "I think just to help students make it in the future, to help students have control over their lives as far as their jobs are concerned. Or if they want to further their education, then they have some sort of background. And that they have become better people hopefully because of me or something that I have said or something that I have done."

Pam: When asked what attracted her to the teaching profession, Pam responded, "Working with kids. History has long been my avocation, and [teaching] was a chance to combine my love of history with love of kids and also the opportunity to do something that is of service. Does that sound too corny? It's true. It's like I spent fourteen to fifteen years pursuing something that was financially very rewarding but wasn't satisfying at all on almost any other level. . . . There is this spiritual component to teaching. I was raised in a very religious household. And in the denomination I was raised in you have an obligation to be of service. I didn't feel like I was fulfilling my obligation to be of service in the business world."

Ruby: When asked what special experience she could identify that prepared her to relate with students the way she does, Ruby responded, "I would say that it was mostly different people in my life that treated me well, that encouraged me to take the next step, to go out and really accomplish what I wanted to do. That really made an impact on me. I was like overwhelmed with 'How do I pay you back? What do I do?' Their comment always was, 'Well, do for someone else someday what we did for you.' It just fit—I am going to do this through education."

Tom: Tom recognizes that during his drug-using and drug-dealing years he hurt many kids. He sees teaching as a way of making amends. "I messed up a lot of people when I was in high school. . . . I believe that life is like a scale of justice. I have a lot of debt on the dark side. Teaching and making a difference in kids' lives helps to balance the scales on my side."

Resource 8

Power of the Position

Dale: "I am entrusted with 150 minds and the professional part of it is that it's my judgment on which way to take those 150 minds for 180 hours. I think that I take that responsibility very heavily. I mean, it's not light. I understand that it's important. I understand that what I say to these kids can go a long way and sometimes I've really got to think about it."

Dean: "I just remember there were educators who really made a difference in my life. A lot of it was how they interacted with me. And I really saw—I mean they could destroy—I watched them destroy some kids, as far as their self-esteem and stuff like that. I'd think, 'Dang! I can't believe this person dogged this person like that!' Or said something that was really hurtful to that individual. 'Oh my God! How could you do that?' It was more of an awareness that I had as I go through life—whether it is in the classroom or dealing with people in general. It is how much power you have just from the words you say, whether you are an educator or not. Words are incredible. They can friggin' destroy people."

Gail: "We have a lot of power, a lot of power. [Teachers] don't realize it until they've done something damaging or until someone has come back after ten years and said, 'I've become this because of you.' I didn't recognize it really, until four years ago when I did an experiment with my class—the blue eyes/brown eyes experiment. It took about seven minutes to make half the kids really mad, really upset, and doubt their abilities. *About seven minutes!* And those are kids that I've had four or five months and just that fast I was able to make them think they were stupid, and they couldn't do well on tests, and the other side of the room was better than they were. It took me another twenty minutes to tell them that this was all a test, not for real."

Pam: "I think that each individual really makes a difference, for one thing. And that the impact that we have on students we might not even begin to understand or realize what that is, but it's there. And it may surface twenty years down the road somewhere for that student. So I think that we have a real moral responsibility to be cognizant of how we treat them all the time. I think the moral dimensions of teaching are really overlooked a lot by teachers and teacher training. But it's such an integral part of what the whole teaching experience is."

Ruby: "You know the little things can really make a difference. A lot of the little things I am not even aware of. Kids will write to me at the end of the year, 'I really appreciated that you did this or that you didn't do this.' Wow! I didn't realize that this was such a noticeable thing.

"It was mostly different educators in my life that treated me well, that encouraged me to take the next step, to go out and really accomplish what I wanted to. It made a big impact on me. I was like overwhelmed with 'How do I pay you back?' Their comment always was, 'Well, do for someone else someday what we did for you.'"

Tom: "I know I've made a difference, you know, in kids. They come back to see me, like the kid yesterday. He's entering the Marines, the music program for the Marines. And yet all he wanted to talk about was his ninth-grade year. You know, and it's scary sometimes to think that you have that much impact. It's terrifying. I'm not real sure a lot of people understand that.

"This is the most important job on the face of the earth. There is nothing more important. There is nothing more important."

Resource 9

Subject as a Vehicle

Dale: "I think I hopefully try to teach more than just math in here. Some of the kids understand that and some don't. I try to teach them what it's like to grow up and to act like adults, although I'm not opposed to them being kids. Just that there are responsibilities that they will need to assume."

Dean: "A kid's got to be able to read; a kid's got to be able to write; a kid's got to be able to do math; but he's also got to be able to work in a group; he's got to be able to respect his peers and deal with people, even people he doesn't like or she doesn't like. They got to be able to have pride in themselves and self-respect and real pride and respect in their community and the people around them. My whole approach to teaching is to take a person and use the academic part to direct all of this—the reading and writing and the math and stuff like that. I use biology like a vehicle to try to make those other things occur, self-respect, all that kind of stuff."

Gail: "I am more interested in self-esteem and happiness first and then the lesson. Because without those two, whatever I teach won't make a difference."

On all three days that I observed Gail, she used her subject matter as a vehicle to guide her students in personal growth. For instance, on day one, the class was reading the story *The Sniper*. In this story, the key characters are enemies. Gail asks the class to reflect on their personal reasons for having enemies. Gail points out that one popular reason for making enemies is jealousy. She illustrates her point by discussing how old movies often have two women fighting over one man. She comments on how insane this behavior is. She coolly suggests, "If a guy doesn't like you, move on to someone who does. Fighting about it will not make him like you."

Pam: "I mean, I love [my content area] and I believe it's real wonderful and all that. But is a seventh grader's life really going to change if they know who the rulers of Mesopotamia are? No. What's more important is that they learn how to be successful as people and they learn how to get along with each other. You know, they learn how to retrieve information that they are going to need. They learn how to work cooperatively. Those are some of the things important to me in teaching kids. That they have a sense of responsibility about being citizens and contributing and about being human beings and having compassion for one another. That's a lot more important to me."

Ruby: "I think that out of all the things that [students] come away with in the classroom, all of the knowledge and skills, I think one of the greatest things that they come away with is just the fact that there's a human being that cares about them. I really think that that makes a difference."

Tom: "I consider myself a very good source of knowledge in terms of history. But at the junior high level, how much of that is really important? It's a drop in the ocean. Everything else is much more important. When you get to the high school level, especially the type that I was dealing with in terms of advanced placement, that knowledge base is much more important. But yet I don't think it's more important than all the other affective things."

Resource 10

Viewing Themselves as Professionals

Dale: "I am entrusted with 150 minds and the professional part of it is that it's my judgment on which way to take those 150 minds for 180 hours. I think that I take that responsibility very heavily. I mean, its not light. I understand that it's important. I understand that what I say to these kids can go a long way and sometimes I've really got to think about it."

Dean: "This is how I view a school. I view a school as a whole bunch of firms, and the classrooms are like a business. I am in charge of the business. I am like the CEO. I am the owner of that business . . . and that is good and bad, because you know why. In order to do that and not become paranoid and weird about it like I see some teachers, you got to have a pretty good ego. You have got to realize that 'I'm alright. I am doing some good stuff.'"

Gail: "I see myself as a professional. I don't have an hourly pay. I am expected to spend time in the office outside of regular time. I have to make decisions about my job. I am able to make decisions about what I want to teach, the grade level, things concerning my job, and how it affects my life. I have a say in what my job is. Someone who is not a professional does not have the freedom to be creative with their job like I do. I do not have to punch a clock."

Pam: "For one thing, not anybody can do this job. It takes training and dedication. And those to me are the hallmarks of professionalism. It also takes a level of integrity and commitment that you don't find in a lot of industries."

Ruby: "I view myself as a professional. I think that we're all clear about what a professional is supposed to do. I think that there's a lot of reform going on with education right now and so what it means to be a teacher might look very different ten years from now."

Tom: "[Teaching] is the most important job on the face of the earth. There's nothing more important. There's nothing more important. There's nothing more important."

Resource 11

Genuineness

Dale: Dale is authentic and genuine with the students. For instance, one student asked him why he always writes two problems on the board for the class to work out rather than one. Dale rolled off a series of reasons, "I am on a role, besides I don't want to break up my thought process and this is easier." Then he paused for a second and said sincerely, "Actually, I don't have a real valid reason." He smiled and so did the students.

Dean: Dean's authenticity is best supported by a parent I spoke with. She said, "He lets his humanity be seen by the kids. I think he does it by being so honest and willing to let people see him make a mistake. He is not afraid to be judged, of messing up in front of people. Kids are not afraid to make a mistake in front of him." Dean says, "No matter what you do you got to be honest. You got to be yourself. You have to show them yourself. Your teaching style has got to be you."

Pam: The day of the discussion on harassment, Pam sent a student, who had picked at a hangnail until it bled, to the nurse's station to get a bandage. She began to joke around about how she hated blood. Several students joined in. They started poking fun at the triviality of the "injury," making fun of the student. Suddenly one student noted that they were harassing the student. "We are doing the very same thing we were talking about." Everyone was immediately quiet. There was a pregnant pause as individuals realized the truth in the statement. Then Pam said, "I was doing it too. What a jerk you have for a teacher!" A student pipes up, "A cool jerk."

Ruby: When asked what she does when she is not in a nurturing mood, Ruby replies, "What I've found works really well is if I'm honest with them. Sometimes if I don't get enough sleep, I can be a little edgy. . . . I'll just tell them, 'You guys, if I appear short today or if

I appear frustrated or whatever, you need to know it's nothing that you've done. I was up real late or I'm not feeling well.' A lot of times they'll be very empathetic back to you."

Tom: Tom's authenticity is evident as he describes his relationship with troubled students. "When I was evaluated, after it was written up, I took it back to class and slapped it on the table. I read it to them, explained what each part meant. So they saw my report card. And so you take it down to where everybody's equal." When asked about the characteristics of a healthy relationship, Tom says, "Well, another is when they can argue with you. Shoot. If they don't argue with you, there's something the matter."

Resource 12

Accountability for Mistakes

Dale: "I kind of like to be able to show the kids—I don't like to prove to the kids how smart I am. If I make a mistake at the board, sometimes I'll do it on purpose to see if they're watching me and sometimes I'll be going too fast and it just happens. And when I do that I go, 'Dang, I made a mistake. I can't believe it!' [said humorously] Like that so it lets you know that I'm a human guy."

From classroom observations: Dale puts a problem on the board for students to figure out. After a few minutes the students start to complain that the problem is impossible. Dale glances at the problem on the board and says, "Oh no! I forgot to carry over." He goes to the board and changes the numbers in the problem. The class groans. "You made a mistake. You are the math teacher. You are supposed to know this stuff." Dale laughs and says, "I made a mistake." Students laugh and tease, "When we make a mistake, you count it against us. How come it doesn't count against you?" Dale teases back, "It does count against me. I have to put up with you guys raggin' on me. Isn't that enough?" The students laugh.

Dean: "I really don't dwell on my mistakes, because what I end up doing is I end up realizing I am going to make a thousand mistakes and just being able to say, 'My fault man, I am sorry. I really shouldn't have gotten in your face like that.' There are times that I push too much. There are times I don't push enough. There are times when I call somebody on something when I shouldn't have because it was really kind of out of pocket for me. You just have to be able to go right up to them and say, 'You know something, I'm sorry.'"

Gail: "I apologized for whatever behavior on my part made that student feel that way. Then she realized that she was being too sensitive, and I realized that I was too. And so we hugged each other and that was it."

From a classroom observation: Several more students walk in. She calls one to the front and tells him she made a mistake on his final grade and she needs to send him down to the office with a grade change form. They tease back and forth.

Pam: "I know one time in the fourth-period class I said something to a student. And I can't remember if it came out wrong or he misunderstood me, but I could see in his face that he thought what he said was stupid. I stopped everything I was doing. And you know, walked over to him and in front of everybody said, 'You know John, it just occurred to me that maybe you think I think that that was a dumb question' or something like that. I don't remember exactly what I said. . . . and he kind of went, 'Well, yeah.' I went, 'Well, that's not what I meant. Let me rephrase what I meant to say to you.' And he just visibly was relieved."

Ruby: "Mistakes are part of life. They're part of the highs and lows of life. . . . That I am not my mistakes . . . that's one I teach to my kids. You know, I am not my mistake. A mistake is an action, not a person. . . . It's okay . . . you're going to come back and try it again, and again, and again."

From a classroom observation: Ruby asks the group if anyone had any questions about where people are. One student said, "You should have asked us earlier so that we had time to think about it." Ruby answers, "Good idea, I will give you time now."

Tom: "I like to tell the kids that I am not perfect. You are not perfect. We're going to make mistakes. I'll tell you when you make one. I hope you tell me when I make one."

Resource 13

Sense of Personal Accountability

Dale: "I used to go out and have a beer or two or three with a lot of the coach guys around here, until about five years ago. Then I decided that that was getting me nowhere. All they do is talk bad about the kids or this and that. I don't need that so I decided—I became so unpopular with the coaches, the older guys, because they didn't invite me to the parties anymore. I mean, they looked down at me for doing that. I felt like an outcast. I could have easily said, 'Hey, I'm going back. I'm going to get back into that group.' But I never did. I just never wanted to do that, I felt that wasn't the right way to go."

Dean: When asked how he handles permission slips, Dean says, "I am bad. I am bad. [laughs] Permission slips are a necessary evil. I do them, but I let kids go on field trips who do not have their full permission slips. . . . It is my choice. Ultimately, if something happened to them and a parent really wanted to be bad, I could probably be reprimanded. I would just say, 'My fault, I thought I had his permission.'" Dean does not blame the student or the school for his decision.

Gail: A student's words best reflect Gail's inner locus of control. When asked what qualities Gail has that she would like to develop, Susan said, "People talk about [Gail] and she does not care. She's like, 'I don't have time to worry about what other people say about me and da-da da da-da.' And I wish I could do that." After lunch, Gail goes to the closet in the back of the room. She freshens up her makeup, lipstick, and mascara. One student comes back and says, "Who are you trying to impress?" She says, "Myself. When you feel good about yourself, you always do a good job."

Pam: Pam does not say the Pledge of Allegiance because it is against her religious principles. She has the kids stand and say it if they wish. She has the boys take off their hats. Pam told me the other teachers give her grief about her stance regarding the pledge and she just shrugs her shoulders. She remains committed to her personal beliefs in the face of colleagues' disapproval.

Ruby: Ruby says, regarding her traumatic childhood, "I don't know where my strength came from, but a lot of things happened to me that could have caused me to make some really bad choices in my life—in high school and earlier. I look at a lot of kids today with some of those same things happening and they have made some bad choices." Ruby refers to an individual's response to traumatic experiences as a choice, including her response.

Tom: When asked what criteria he uses to define himself as a professional, Tom said, "That is an interesting question. One is the ability to be self-directed, to be a part of the solution, to be a part of the long-range plan."

As a social activist, Tom works hard to bring about change in situations he sees as inequitable or inadequate. Tom says, "I'm always trying to learn new things and new ways. Figuring out different ways of doing things. I'm willing to risk doing things the unconventional way. Let parents get mad. It's good for them if it brings them into the school."

Resource 14

Nonjudgmental Stance

Dale: "He is really caring about people. He's not judgmental about people. You know, he doesn't judge them by the way they look or anything. He just cares about the personality and the way—he can see what's inside the person."

Twenty minutes late, Joe walks into class. Earlier students had wagered bets that Joe would not make it to one class on time this week. Dale nods recognition of Joe and says, "Tough weekend, huh Joe?" Joe nods and finds his seat. Later, Joe walks across the front of the room to throw something in the wastebasket. Dale says quietly, "Hi buddy." Joe says, "How are you doing?" Dale says, "I am having a rough morning." Joe says, "Me too!" and returns to his seat.

Dean: Dean had asked his TA to clean dead fish and dirty water from a fish tank in the back of the room. The TA refused to do the nasty task but Dean insisted, explaining to her that it was her responsibility. She tackled the task halfheartedly during Dean's lunch hour. After about half an hour, with the tank still half full of water, the TA left the room and did not return. Water was splashed everywhere within a radius of three feet. Dean returned from lunch and asked if the TA left because she got sick from the smell. He laughed and then expressed pleasure over how well she had done with emptying the tank. He looked in the tank and said again, "She did really well, really well." Dean sees what the TA did right, not what she did wrong.

Gail: When asked how she handles a student who keeps promising to do his or her homework but comes to class every day with excuses, Gail responds, "Well, I try to figure out, maybe, if I am giving this person too much to do. Or if this person has outside interests that are taking over his or her time. . . . Maybe this person can't read and is in the tenth or eleventh grade without anyone knowing that this person cannot read. And that does happen because people who can't read have mastered fooling people. They can get by. It takes a while for you to realize that a person cannot read or a person is not comfortable with reading and does not do the work." Notice that Gail first thinks of barriers for the student rather than assuming resistant and inappropriate behavior on the student's part.

Pam: "I think for a lot of these students, you know, this is a period in their lives when they are going to test boundaries constantly. And what I have to always do is be real clear about what my boundaries are and have them be reasonable and have them be something that an adolescent can understand and relate to about the whys of it and not just sound arbitrary. I convey to them right up front right away, 'I'm trying to be reasonable with you as I would want you to be with me.' And just tell them that and speak straight from the heart."

Ruby: Ruby asks the class, "What do you think that I will not let you put on the collage?" A student says, "Tobacco and alcohol." Ruby pauses and says, "Other students have said that but I let students do that because if that is really important to them then they need to express that." One student replies, "Sick!" Ruby says, "Well, how else can we say that without putting people down?" She says, "People need to feel free to express who they are. That is where their lives are at this time."

Tom: "I had a girl early this year who I was concerned about because she was so solemn and withdrawn. . . . She's completely different, and she just had never felt comfortable and wasn't—you know, she didn't feel like she was the best at the subject matter. I said, 'Hey, if you could just give me what you consider to be your best shot at something and you can tell me that you tried your hardest, you'll do okay. You'll do okay in here too.' She responded real well."

Resource 15

Humor

Dale: Another faculty member walks into the classroom. Dales says, "Ladies and gentlemen, Mr. Stewart. One courtesy clap." The students all clap once in unison. Mr. Stewart smiles broadly. He came to take the VCR.

Students walk in and ask, "What are we doing today?" Dale answers, "We have to do fractions today . . . the 'F' word." Students moan, "Oh no, the 'F' word." They work on fractions. Dale says, "You guys are geniuses!" A student says, "Tell my mom that." Dales says, "You want me to? She'll believe me." Another student says, "She'd probably get you fired." Dale responded hopelessly, "I looked at my bank statement this weekend, and I've got to keep working."

Dean: After working several minutes with two students who were teaming on a project, Dean said to one student in the dyad study group, "Does your back hurt?" Both students looked at him somewhat confused. "My back hurt? What do you mean?" the one student said. Dean replied, "From carrying him through his assignment." Both students laughed.

Gail: Gail asks the students what they would do if they went home today and found they had been evicted from their home. Someone mentions they would rob an old lady. Gail hoots and says, "I take offense at that!" Then she adds, "You would have a permanent place to stay then, and you wouldn't have to worry about meals either!" She asks them the next question. "What if you go home and find that your parents are unemployed?" A group of students groan and mumble something about "as if their parents worked in the first place!" Gail rephrases the question. "OK. You lose whatever source of income you have." Another student mentions something illegal. Gail says, "You'll have a job, a job making license plates."

Pam: When Pam was facilitating the discussion on harassment, she flashed, "I feel like Oprah Winfrey!" and she proceeded into a short impromptu vignette of Oprah. She raced up and down the aisles, holding a make-believe microphone under the chins of different students while she facetiously asked questions.

Ruby: One student asked how she could make up the work from yesterday. Apparently they did role plays with each other on healthy ways to express anger. Ruby says, "Shall we make her do a one-person skit?" The class shouts, "Yes!" The student laughs because she knows Ruby is teasing.

    One kid says, "That sucks!" Ruby stops and says, "We don't say that word in here." The students says, "We don't?" Ruby responds, "No, we say Hoover or vacuum." The students laugh.

Resource 16

Effective Communication Skills

Dale: "I think that the thing I try to do there is to stop, and if they want to talk, let them talk. If they want to hold it, then that's their choice, too. I just think that in the past when the kids come to me and talk to me, they know they can open up and say some things. There have been some things I wish some kids had not said. They've told me some things—but you can't . . . once you're there, you're there. I try to direct them to the right [person]."

Dean: A students says, "He listens, and he doesn't get excited enough to get all angry at you or nothing. He'll just help you try to figure out a way to solve that problem."

Gail: "I think I'm a good listener, and I think I know when to give advice and when to listen."

Pam: A student says, "I had this thing going on with the school and stuff, and this one girl thought we did something but we didn't do any of it. Me and my friends, we did something . . . we really didn't. I didn't want to talk to the counselor, because the counselor was, like, all on their side and so he wouldn't even listen to us. So then, [Pam] said I could talk to her and then I just went and talked to her. And it helped."

Ruby: "I think to give kids time to be listened to is important . . . to give back to them 'this is what I heard you saying' or pull out a little bit of the phrase that they're giving the answer to and have them explain that a little bit more. Once again, just to give them the opportunity to talk about things."

Tom: "You don't have to have the answers. All they wanted to do was have somebody to talk to . . . who will listen to them instead of listening while they are doing something else. They can get anybody to listen while they are doing something else, but to really just sit and listen with undivided attention, that's something else all together."

Resource 17

Conflict Resolution Skills

Dale: "I'll ask them what's the problem. I'll get two different stories and then I'll try to go in and determine what really went on and the reason behind this. A lot of times it's real minor and the kids get all upset right away, so then I'll call them up and I'll talk to them—separate of course."

Dean: "Yesterday there was a major conflict. And those things . . . I resolve conflicts all the time. Two kids coming up and they are like talking . . . a head mounting. 'Hey! You got to come on. You guys need to chill.' Or whatever, I just resolve conflict all the time."

Gail: "I take the student that is least resistant away from it or tell them to take it somewhere else, choose another time or another place and another time. And if it is directed toward me, I use a little bit of humor sometimes, then just kind of play it off and talk to them later because I really haven't sent them to the office in a while. . . . If it is students I don't know, then I'll try to call somebody else first because sometimes it is kind of hard to get involved when you don't know the students, you don't know what is happening."

Pam: "I think if a student is having a problem, like kids will swear in my class and they just don't seem to think twice about it. Some of them become very surprised when I will hold them accountable for it. 'That is not okay to do in my class because it's very offensive to many people.' Again, we just try to handle that one-on-one. When I deal with a kid with a conflict, because sometimes they will take it personally, or whatever, I will try to go out of my way to find them doing something right in the next little while and acknowledge that to them."

Ruby: "[I] deal with that student one-on-one and find out where the concern is, where the problem was, or where the lack of understanding was and try to paraphrase it and really focus in on where the lack of understanding came from and why."

Tom: "There is a lot of negative feeling between us [a student and Tom] right now. How do I deal with it? I basically ignore it at this point, right now. I let them kind of go through their feelings and a lot of times I'll sit back and kind of wait to see if they're going to take the first step forward. . . . I usually let it go about three days and if they don't make contact then it's usually me that does and I just give them the chance. I'll start out with, 'Okay, what are you angry with me about?' and I let them speak their mind first. . . . We go from there."

References

Aspy, D. N., & Roebuck, F. N. (1972). An investigation of the relationship between levels of cognitive functioning and the teacher's classroom behavior. *Journal of Educational Research, 65,* 365–368.

Baumrind, D. (1971a). Current patterns of parental authority. *Developmental Psychology Monographs, 4*(1, Pt. 2).

Baumrind, D. (1971b). Harmonious parents and their preschool children. *Developmental Psychology, 4,* 99–102.

Benard, B. (1991, August). *Fostering resiliency in kids: Protective factors in the family, school, and community.* Washington, DC: Department of Education. (ERIC Document Reproduction Service No. ED335781).

Bennis, W. G., Schein, E. H., Steele, F. I., & Berlew, D. (1968). *Interpersonal dynamics: Essays and readings on human interaction* (2nd ed.). Homewood, IL: The Dorsey Press.

Bowlby, J. (1988). *A secure base.* New York: Basic Books.

Briggs, D. C. (1977). *Celebrate yourself.* Garden City, NY: Doubleday.

Bronfenbrenner, U. (1986, February). Alienation and the four worlds of childhood. *Phi Delta Kappan, 67,* 430–435.

Brook, J. S., Brook, D. W., Gordon, A. S., Whiteman, M., & Cohen, P. (1990). The psychosocial etiology of adolescent drug use: A family interactional approach. *Genetic, Social, and General Psychology Monograph, 116*(2), 111–267.

Carkhuff, R. R. (1969). *Helping and human relations: A primer for lay and professional helpers* (Vol. 1). New York: Holt, Rinehart & Winston.

Carkhuff, R. R. (1987). *The art of helping VI* (6th ed.). Amherst, MA: Resource Development Press.

Cole, M., & Cole, S. R. (1989). *The development of children.* New York: Scientific American Books.

Coleman, J. S. (1974). *Youth: Transitions to adulthood.* Chicago: University of Chicago Press.

Coleman, J. S. (1985, April). Schools and the communities they serve. *Phi Delta Kappan, 66,* 527–532.

Corey, M., & Corey, G. (2002). *Groups: Process and practice* (6th ed.). Pacific Grove, CA: Brooks/Cole.

Deiro, J. (1994). *What teachers do to nurture bonding with students.* Unpublished doctoral dissertation, University of Washington, Seattle.

Deiro, J. (1996). *Teaching with heart: Making healthy connections with students.* Thousand Oaks, CA: Corwin Press.

Dolezal, S. E., Welsh, L., Pressley, M., & Vincent, M. (2003). How nine third-grade teachers motivate student academic engagement. *Elementary School Journal, 103*(3), 239–267.

Edelwich, J., & Brodsky, A. (1980). *Burn-out: Stages of disillusionment in the helping professions*. New York: Human Sciences Press.

Erwin, J. C. (2003). Giving students what they need. *Educational Leadership, 61*(1), 19–23.

Farber, B. A. (1991). *Crisis in education: Stress and burnout in the American teacher*. San Francisco: Jossey-Bass.

Fielding, M. (1982, April). *Personality and situational correlates of teacher stress and burnout*. Paper presented at the American Educational Research Association, New York.

French, J. R., & Raven, B. (1959). The bases of social power. In D. Cartwright (Ed.), *Studies in social power* (pp. 150–167). Ann Arbor, MI: Institute for Social Research.

Glenn, H. S. (1989). *Introduction to developing capable young people* [Videotape]. Fair Oaks, CA: Sunrise Productions.

Glenn, H. S. (1996). Developing capable young people: The leader's guide. In *Developing capable young people* (pp. 159). Fair Oaks, CA: Sunrise Books, Tapes, and Videos.

Glenn, H. S., & Nelsen, J. (1988). *Raising self-reliant children in a self-indulgent world*. Rocklin, CA: Prima Publishing & Communications.

Goodlad, J. I. (1990). *Teachers for our nation's schools*. San Francisco: Jossey-Bass.

Goodman, J. F., Sutton, V., & Harkavy, I. (1995). The effectiveness of family workshops in a middle school setting: Respect and caring make the difference. *Phi Delta Kappan, 76*(9), 694–700.

Hall, P. H. N. (2003). Building relationships with challenging children. *Educational Leadership, 61*(1), 60–63.

Hawkins, J. D., Catalano, R., & Miller, J. Y. (1992). Risk and protective factors for alcohol and other drug problems in adolescence and early adulthood: Implications for substance abuse prevention. *Psychological Bulletin, 112*(2), 64–105.

Heifetz, L. J., & Bersani, H. A. J. (1983). Disrupting the cybernetics of personal growth: Toward a unified theory of burnout in the human services. In B. A. Farber (Ed.), *Stress and burnout in the human service professions* (pp. 46–62). Elmsford, NY: Pergamon Press.

Heller, K. (1989). The return to community. *American Journal of Community Psychology, 17*(1), 1–15.

Herr, N. (2001). Television. *The Sourcebook for Teaching Science*. Retrieved April, 2004, from www.csun.edu/~vceed002/health/docs/tv&health.html

Hoffman, D., & Levak, B. (2003). Personalizing schools. *Educational Leadership, 61*(1), 30–34.

Hoffman, M. L. (1970). Conscience, personality, and socialization techniques. *Human Development, 13*, 90–126.

Hurn, C. J. (1985). *The limits and possibilities of schooling: An introduction to the sociology of education* (2nd ed.). Boston: Allyn & Bacon.

Johnson, D. W. (1972). *Reaching out*. Englewood Cliffs, NJ: Prentice Hall.

Jourard, S. (1964). *The transparent self*. Princeton, NJ: Van Nostrand Reinhold.

Karen, R. (1990, February). Becoming attached. *The Atlantic Monthly*, 35–70.

Kidder, T. (1990). *Among school children*. Boston: Houghton Mifflin.

Kubey, R., & Csikszentmihalyi, M. (1990). *Television and the quality of life: How viewing shapes everyday experiences*. Hillsdale, NJ: Lawrence Erlbaum.

Ladson-Billings, G. (1992). Reading between the lines and beyond the pages: A culturally relevant approach to literacy teaching. *Theory Into Practice, 31*(4), 312–320.

Lieberman, A., & Miller, L. (1984). *Teachers, their world, and their work*. Alexandria, VA: Association for Supervision and Curriculum Development.

Main, M., Kaplan, N., & Cassidy, J. (1985). Security in infancy, childhood, and adulthood: A move to the level of representation. In I. Bretherton & E. Waters (Eds.), *Growing points of attachment theory and research, Monograph of the Society for Research in Child Development 50*(1–2, Serial No. 209), 66–104.

Marlin, T. R. (1987). *Teacher burnout and locus-of-control, sex, age, marital status, and years of experience among a group of urban secondary teachers*. New Brunswick, NJ: Rutgers University.

Marzano, R. J., & Marzano, J. S. (2003). The key to classroom management. *Educational Leadership, 61*(1), 6–13.

McDermott, R. P. (1977). Social relations as context for learning. *Harvard Educational Review, 47*, 198–213.

McIntyre, T. (1984). The relationship between locus of control and teacher burnout. *British Journal of Educational Psychology, 54*(2), 235–238.

McLaughlin, M., & Talbert, J. (1990). Constructing a personalized school environment. *Phi Delta Kappan, 72*(3), 230–235.

McNabb, W. H. (1990). *The developing capable people parenting course: A study of its impact on family cohesion*. Unpublished doctoral dissertation, Pepperdine University, Malibu, CA.

Mendes, E. (2003). What empathy can do. *Educational Leadership, 61*(1), 56–59.

Moskovitz, S. (1983). *Love despite hate: Child survivors of the Holocaust and their adult lives*. New York: Schocken.

Noblit, G. W., Rogers, D. L., & McCadden, B. M. (1995). In the meantime the possibilities of caring. *Phi Delta Kappan, 76*(9), 680–685.

Noddings, N. (1988, December 7). Schools face crisis in caring. *Education Week,* p. 10.

Noddings, N. (1992). *The challenge to care in schools*. New York: Teachers College Press.

O'Donnell, J., Hawkins, D., Catalano, R., Abbott, R. D., & Day, L. E. (1995, January). Preventing school failure, drug use, and delinquency among low-income children: Long-term intervention in elementary schools. *American Journal of Orthopsychiatry, 65*(1), 87–100.

Peck, M. S. (1987). *The different drum: Community making and peace*. New York: Simon & Schuster.

Pedersen, E., Faucher, T. A., & Eaton, W. W. (1978). The new perspective on the effects of first-grade teachers on children's subsequent adult status. *Harvard Educational Review, 48*(1), 1–31.

Rist, R. (1970). Social class and teacher expectations: The self-fulfilling prophecy in ghetto education. *Harvard Educational Review, 40*, 411–451.

Rogers, C. (1961). *On becoming a person*. Boston: Houghton Mifflin.

Rogers, C., Gendlin, E., Keisler, D., & Truax, C. (1967). *Therapeutic relationship and its impact*. Westport, CT: Greenwood.

Rogers, D., & Webb, J. (1991). The ethics of caring in teacher education. *Journal of Teacher Education, 42*(3), 173–181.

Rothman, R. (1992). Study 'from inside' finds a deeper set of school problems. *Education Week, 12*(13), 1–9.

Rutter, M. (1987). Continuities and discontinuities from infancy. In J. D. Osafsky (Ed.), *Handbook of infant development* (2nd ed.) (pp. 1256–1296). Oxford: Oxford University Press.

Small, J. (1981). *Becoming naturally therapeutic* (2nd ed.). Austin, TX: The Eupsychian Press.

Weinstein, C. S. (1998). I want to be nice, but I have to be mean. *Teaching and Teacher Education, 14*(2), 153–163.

Wentzel, K. R. (1997). Student motivation in middle school: The role of perceived pedagogical caring. *Journal of Educational Psychology, 89*(3), 411–419.

Werner, E. E., & Smith, R. S. (1992). *Overcoming the odds: High risk children from birth to adulthood*. Ithaca, NY: Cornell University Press.

Wiggins, J. D. (1982). Improving student behaviors with Carkhuff-model counseling. *School Counselor, 30*(1), 57–60.

Wolk, S. (2003). Hearts and minds. *Educational Leadership, 61*(1), 14–18.

Index

CORWIN PRESS

The Corwin Press logo—a raven striding across an open book—represents the union of courage and learning. Corwin Press is committed to improving education for all learners by publishing books and other professional development resources for those serving the field of K–12 education. By providing practical, hands-on materials, Corwin Press continues to carry out the promise of its motto: **"Helping Educators Do Their Work Better."**